Gateway ̶̶̶
Adventures of another gr
a shaman

Nathan D. Horowitz

The *Nighttime Daydreams* quadrilogy is:

Gateway Mexico (First and Second Journeys)

Bat Dreams (Third and Fourth Journeys)

Provisional Truths (First Part of Fifth Journey)

Beyond Wahuya (Second Part of Fifth Journey and Epilogue)

Collect them all!

Previous versions of portions of these texts have appeared in *Ashé*, *The Cenacle*, *Dragibus*, *Driesch*, *Psychedelic Press UK*, and *Qarrtsiluni*, and on the forums at Ayahuasca.com. Half of the author's post-tax royalties are earmarked for the Siekopai (Secoya) nation of Ecuador in return for their allowing their myths and legends to appear in *Nighttime Daydreams*.

These books are dedicated to my daughter Livia, in hopes that she won't read them until she's much older.

Table of Contents

No physician gives medicine to the healthy.
I will become all pain, if I must,
to be given the Remedy.
Rumi

1. The Author Decides to End it All

Moonless, clear night, northern Michigan, February, 1985, frozen lake glowing dully, snow crystals reflecting the Milky Way. A hundred-foot-wide spiral is developing on the surface of the lake, curving clockwise toward its center. Inscribing it with his shuffling feet is a tall, gangly, white teenager. Navy blue down jacket, leather Patagonia hiking boots, gray wool cap with a *Greenpeace* patch sewn on. Wide green eyes and a small chin give him the look of a hairless cat.

The boy's lips are moving. What's he saying?

"...*Gi, go, gi, go, gi, go....*"

Chanting to the rhythm of his steps, he shuffles through four inches of powder snow and starlight atop the ice. Left foot *gi*, right foot *go*. Bootsoles don't leave the ice. *Gi, go, gi, go.* An acronym from computing: garbage in, garbage out. The quality of the input determines the quality of the output. *This explains my life,* he's thinking. *What can be expected of me, if the input was so bad?*

He's drawing the gigo spiral both as a landscape-art piece (homage to Robert Smithson's 1972 *Spiral Jetty*) and as a signal for help to whatever God or gods might deign to glance down.

Sucking the freezing air into his lungs, trying to stare into the future as the seers of old were said to have done, he feels the closeness of the spirit world, but he can't reach it. Recently turned seventeen, he's the most intelligent and most fucked-up person in the world. He wants to fly up and dissolve in the cold wind that glides without thinking above the frozen land. His body can't support the transformations he wishes to undergo. Therefore, he would like to die.

To die. That's what Elena wanted. Or didn't want. She's with her family in Miami now. In the middle of the night, she stood in her shower with a razor blade pressed against her wrist. Finally decided to withdraw from the school instead, leaving him without her mad mind that matched his own.

Every time he goes inside himself, all he feels is pain. It's the core of his being. If he were different, he could get it out by hurting people. Punching someone. Joining the military and killing people in foreign lands. Or getting a pistol and shooting his classmates. Each bullet that left the barrel would pull one nail out of his heart.

But any time he's ever hurt someone, he's ended up feeling worse than they did. So he's left with no one to harm but himself. He thinks again about jumping off the balcony in his dorm and breaking his leg. The pain would give his mind some clarity. Or shooting himself in the forehead. One blast and all the thoughts would be gone.

He's convinced if he survives to adulthood he'll be a great poet. All the signs are there. He's lonely and sensitive. No one really understands him. He feels more intensely and thinks more deeply than other people. He's willing to endure the suffering he knows the muse requires. The words of the poets who came before him are flare guns burning holes in his darkness. From the history of literature, he has inherited hundreds of barrels of rusty symbolism. And he can turn a phrase, turn it into a lion, scratch it under the chin so it purrs, dissolve it in a shower of sparks.

He trudges on, *gi, go, gi, go*, breath-plumes lit by stars and snow.

Here in northern Michigan, at Interbergen School for the Arts, the boy majors in creative writing. He's no good at short stories—can't imagine plots or characters ("There's no narrative drive here," the fiction teacher said)—but he can take a thought and coat it with words, and let that dry, and peel it off, and that's a poem. "By the time you're twenty-one," the poetry teacher said, "you'll be publishing in the best journals in the country."

And despite his psychological problems, for the first time, he's one of the popular kids. Maybe because everyone's a bit mad here. It's all the art that does it. Or the sunless winter. Some girls even like him. Maybe because at close range, he smells of mad genius. Maybe they'd like to be able to say, decades later, "I messed around with the famous poet when he was a crazy young man." Or maybe they just like him.

But it's not easy for him to see why. Since he was thirteen, the inside of his head has been like a Stephen King novel about Hieronymus Bosch and the Marquis de Sade on vacation in Auschwitz. The boy didn't ask for sick thoughts. Doesn't want them. Can't drive them away. They live under his roof like a nest of flies. He's almost gotten used to their buzzing songs about rotting and shit. He thinks they may even be the real him. They tell him to hurt people. They tell him he'll like it. He figures they're the spawn of the rage and jealousy he feels toward normal people—happy people; stupid,

7

sleeping people—whose souls weren't ripped in half when they were four. Visions of torture swarm him like fanged, beaked demons around Saint Anthony in the Renaissance paintings his dad showed him in museums.

So will he be the crunchy prey of madness? The next Charlie Manson, Jack the Ripper? *I'd rather die,* the boy swears as he gigos forward, seeing his tall, gangly body lying in a coffin, dressed in a dark blue suit. His dad's brother and sister hold up their collapsing brother. His mom wails in her grim second husband's arms. Womb to tomb, baby. *Gi, go, gi, go.*

What keeps the boy alive? Literature and lovemaking. The first time he and Elena did it, he couldn't believe anyone had ever enjoyed it as much as they did. Afterwards, breathing each other's breath, they cuddled like Adam and Eve, sweat and brown hair mixed and mashed on their pressed-together foreheads.

But now she's gone, and most days, he feels like screaming.

He reaches the center of his spiral, pulls off his mittens, jams them in the pockets of his navy blue down jacket. Wind whistles and moans.

If I shot myself in the forehead now, he thinks, *the wound would become another whistle, a clean, empty hole moaning in the wind.*

He reaches for the sky and silently begs the winking stars to take him out of this dream.

When they don't, and when he's done feeling the cold air whip across his hands, he quietly retraces his spiraling steps and heads for the dorm, and Brubaker.

Vibram soles, car-tire-black with a thin line of yellow, trickle snow-melt on the doormat. Crosslegged on his bed, cheeks flushed, the boy holds his icy toes in his hands to warm them through damp socks. A dim smell of wool and foot. For a few moments, the only sound is the punk song on his roommate's stereo: guitar, bass, drum kit, an incoherent shouting. Then Brubaker erupts: "She didn't want to *kill* herself! If she *had,* she would have *done* it, instead of just *talking* about it. Speaking of talking, you're a pretty good talker. Why don't you talk some sense into your head?"

Quarrelsome/haughty/sad/pissed off/convinced he's right, the boy stares at the floor and chokes out, "Everything *I've* heard about people who commit suicide says that they sometimes *do* talk about it, so if anyone ever says they're *contemplating suicide"*—his voice trembles— "you should take that *really* seriously. I'll tell you right now, *I'm* thinking of killing *my*self, and the fact that I'm telling you is no guarantee I won't."

Brubaker shakes his head. "That's bullshit and you fuckin' know it! Nat, man, I know your parents have you convinced you're a genius. You're their only kid. I get that. But if you are, you're the *dumbest* goddamned genius I've ever met! Plenty of geniuses walking around here are a hell of a lot smarter than you."

Leaving the damp footprints of a genius or madman, the boy stalks into the bathroom. Fills an empty Sprite can from the tap. Takes a bottle of aspirin out of the medicine chest. Stares for a second in the mirror at his own eyes like green and black pills.

He plunks back down on his bed, unscrews the childproof cap, plucks out the cotton, shakes a white tablet onto the moist palm of his left hand. The music has ended, and the room is quiet save for the humming of amplifiers and of the fluorescent lights above the boys' desks.

"I'm gonna fuckin' end this," he tells Brubaker in the sudden stillness. "Right now."

His roommate watches him gulp the first aspirin with a swig of water. Then the second, then the third.

But ultimately, Brubaker's right: he doesn't quite want to die. After twenty, he smacks can and bottle on his desk, saying, "Now go get whoever's on duty! They have to drive me to the hospital! Go!"

A thirtysomething doctor with a broad, brown beard gives him a blue hospital gown, a little bottle labeled Syrup of Ipecac, and a huge steel bowl to vomit in. The boy screams bile into the concave mirror. When it's over, his and the doctor's eyes meet. The doctor seems to see some value in him that he doesn't see in himself, and with his eyes, asks him not to do anything like this again. At the same time, the doctor looks as if he'd love to beat the hell out of whatever's harming the boy, if only he knew how.

2. Research Questions and Methodology

Twenty aspirins was the sweet spot: not enough to cause me permanent damage, if only because I got treated fast, but enough to convince everyone I was serious, whatever the hell I was up to.

My stepdad drove the rust-colored Chevy Nomad station wagon north all night from Ann Arbor, somberly collected me at dawn in the school infirmary, drove me home.

Three weeks of therapy, then back to the academy. Everyone, including Brubaker, was nice to me. I'd expressed the desperation they felt, too, for their respective reasons. They'd all died-and-been-reborn a bit. They were also just glad I hadn't actually killed myself. Fighting shadows of their own, they understood me, or had caught, at least, a glimpse.

In a book in the library, I read about a psychedelic potion used in shamanic rituals in the Amazon: *ayahuasca*—the name meant vine of the soul, vine of the dead, vine of the spirits.

It was like the peyote cactus in the Castaneda books, accounts of a sorcerer's apprenticeship in Mexico. When I'd read them in junior high, those books had made more sense to me than science or religion did. At age thirteen, when other kids were focused on preparing for bar mitzvahs, or roller skating to disco music, or playing football, I wanted to visit separate realities.

At sixteen, I'd dropped acid in downtown Ann Arbor with my friend Murray. Our ouroboros dialog wove in and out between time and infinity.

11

Japanese exchange students' white t-shirts turned a neon pink that bled several inches into the air. At night, the red throb of a blinking stoplight was pleasure, love, sorrow. Around a star at the top of the sky, a rose bloomed. Amazing. I wanted more.

But afterwards, I became wary of going out of my mind in the city. One of our classmates, in fact, would die a year later in a car crash on acid.

Now I thought the jungle would be a good place to trip, though it was impossibly far away.

I read on. Soul-vine drinkers puked and saw kaleidoscope designs and snakes and jaguars. The spirit of the potion was supposed to be a rainbow-colored serpent.

Vomiting with the syrup of ipecac had rid me of a tiny fraction of the psychological garbage I'd been carrying around. I'd felt lighter afterwards, and, indeed, less bat-shit crazy. Maybe I could have done more, I thought now, if I'd been tripping at the same time, and been helped by a professional healer—and a rainbow serpent in whose existence I wondered if I could believe.

The book went on about shamans. Long ago, their magical speech had given rise to poetry. They could send their souls out of their bodies. They fought one another with spells. They could see inside their patients' bodies and pull sickness out with their hands, or suck it out with their mouths.

Because I found it hard to believe in anything, I wondered how the shamans and the people around them could convince themselves of those experiences. To me, raised sort of Jewish, sort of atheist, nothing was certain, no truth was given or obvious. *Who and what are we? Where were we before we were conceived? Where do we go when we die? What about sex and sexuality, what are those all about? What are good and evil, and how can we be good? Can we stop hurting each other? Can we stop destroying the Earth? Do indigenous people know anything that can help the rest of us? What are spirits? Why do the myths I read ring so true? Why do people believe in one God, or many, or none? How do individuals and cultures determine their beliefs? How do those beliefs change? Are our beliefs going to keep on changing forever?*

A few of my weed experiences had been strong enough to temporarily shut down my questioning, which had come as a huge relief. Maybe ayahuasca could rest my mind by letting me believe in something, even if only for a while. Even if it wasn't real. *What is real?*

I read of a common way people enter the shaman profession. A kid is sick for a long time. A diagnosis—by a shaman, naturally—finds that the illness is caused by spirits who will cure the kid if he or she becomes a shaman. The parents give their approval and the illness passes.

My gaze flicked up from the book through a floor-to-ceiling window at a grove of pines. Under the churning gray sky, the snow on the branches looked like Italian marble. It ought to be melting soon. But the days were still cold. Maybe I'd found my problem. Maybe I was getting worked over by spirits who would quit hassling me if I learned to work with them. Maybe I could go to a shaman and be healed and become a shaman myself.

But as I lay in bed that night listening to my friend Brubaker softly snoring, I knew I'd never be a shaman. I'd been born in the wrong culture. Realistically, I'd probably be a poet in New York, part of a literary movement like the Dadaists, the Surrealists, or the Beats. I also imagined I could fly a single-engine plane smuggling pot out of Colombia into the United States. That was just a private joke, though: it sounded fun, but it wasn't something I'd really do. In junior high, I'd taken a standardized career test that found I was suited to be a museum curator. Sure, why not? The Museum of Natural History in my hometown was an interdimensional gateway to distant times and places; it appeared in my dreams with strange architectures and exhibits. In real life, its motto was chiseled in sandstone above the entrance: "Go to Nature; take the facts into your own hands; look, and see for yourself."

The thought of working in an office from nine to five gave me chest pain. And I vowed I wouldn't teach at colleges, like my parents and my stepdad did. I wished I could go to Nature and take the facts into my hands.

I thought about the cold wind slipping over the dormitory in darkness, and soon I was asleep.

3. The Call to Adventure

I followed the rump of Jennifer's blue jeans with my eyes till the screen door of Kosher Co-op banged shut. She'd broken up with me two weeks before, but we were still friends. This meant we usually had lunch together, and I tried to get her back into bed. That never worked.

I contemplated the *National Geographic* magazine on the table in front of me, its cover photo of a lionfish in dark water—barbed, quill-like, rainbow-colored fins fanning out around the baleful face.

I was in my last semester at a small liberal arts college in Ohio. To disguise its identity, let's call it Berlino. I was an English major with a subconcentration in Creative Writing and a minor in Religion. For four years, I'd nourished myself on great books—*Canterbury Tales, Ulysses, My Life in the Bush of Ghosts*—while pacing up and down in what felt like an expensive cage. I'd been guided by my mom to a highly-rated private institution, toward graduate school and an academic career. As the semesters rolled by, I still didn't know what *I* wanted to do when I got out. I only knew I didn't want to go for a Master's or a PhD. Academia felt like living inside a condom. I wanted to touch life. I loved my girlfriends, one after another, but couldn't give myself to any of them. I remembered the book about shamans. I thought nature was trying to say something to me, or the spirits were, but there was too much noise in my life to hear. I loved literature, but I didn't want to be only a reader and a writer. I wanted to be a hero in my own adventure. That didn't seem to be an option, though. So I traveled in books. They were spaceships, time machines, multipliers of identity.

Unlike those at the arts academy, my writing teachers here were unanimously unimpressed with my poetry and repelled by my inflated opinion of it. I, in turn, pitied them for not being as successful as I was sure I'd be at their age. I kept writing but stopped showing my work to them. Writing had become something I did reflexively, like nail-biting, foot-tapping, and certain other things that people do. Sometimes I wrote out of joy, too, and then it was like tattooing the skin of the earth with lightning.

Keeping the unspoken promise I'd made to the doctor, I no longer considered killing myself. But I had constant pain in my lower back. I was sure there was nothing wrong with me physically except what was wrong with me mentally: trauma from my parents' divorce and their years-long custody battle over me. But I couldn't take that garbage out. Its putrescent vapors gave me waking nightmares.

In my first semester at Berlino, I'd tried to redeem myself by giving some rein to my dark impulses. After all, they were natural. Atavistic. The key was to channel them into something positive. *Love.* Her eyes downcast, the blonde girl with the flute flashed through my mind. Even after four years, my cheeks flushed.

On the opposite wall was an oil stain where I'd thrown a fried chicken thigh during a food fight with the rabbi. Below the stain, a sparsely-mustached stranger was gesturing broadly as he

16

conversed with friends of mine. He seemed to know them. He'd probably graduated and was visiting. Though it was warm in the co-op, he wore a brightly-colored Andean Inca knit cap with ear flaps and tassels.

My 9:00 class that day had been Archaeology of the Ancient Maya. Professor Salguera had lectured on the *Popol Vuh*, the holy book of the Quiché Maya. "They called it an instrument of seeing," she had purred in her Cuban lilt. "It presented mythology that transported them imaginatively to primordial times; but, equally, it was part of their divination system. It gave them information beyond what their senses could ordinarily receive. In that way, it allowed them to approach the condition of their all-seeing ancestors. You see, as the *Popol Vuh* relates, the gods created the first four men with senses that were infinite. They could see, hear, smell, taste, and feel everything in the world at once." She paused, tipped her pretty head to the side, smiled. "The gods decided these men were too powerful, and they limited their senses to what we have now. But they gave them gifts to make up for it: women— and books, instruments of seeing."

I looked back at the oil stain on the wall— an asymmetrical Rorschach blot—another instrument of seeing. Didn't look like a book, though. More like an island. Or a dolphin. I'd learned in Surrealism class that the French poet Arthur Rimbaud had recommended finding images in random forms in the environment, such as a mosque in a cloud. "One must become a seer," the teen visionary had added, "through a systematic

17

derangement of all the senses." Rimbaud was like
The Little Prince on acid and with gangrene in one
leg.

*Maybe the dolphin and the island are symbols of my
future,* I thought. *I'd like to pull a Rimbaud and leave
civilization behind. Go to an island and swim with dolphins.
But when I graduate, I'm just gonna move back in with my
mom and stepdad and live in my forest-green bedroom at the
northwest corner of the second floor of their house. I'll find a
meaningless job, systematically derange my senses, and plan
my next move. Maybe I'll go to Japan and teach English
and study Butoh dance. Anything to get out of the States.*

I made eye contact with the lionfish. I'd
brought the magazine to help explain psychedelics
to my friend Ben, who disapproved of them,
without, I felt, knowing enough about them. But
Ben hadn't shown up to lunch. A week earlier, I'd
picked up this issue—October, 1990—from my
mailbox while on mushrooms. *When I emerge into the
sunlight, the central quadrangle is filled with soft,
transparent spheres. I curl up with the magazine in a big
wrought-iron chair and marvel at the lionfish, whose face
looks like Bob Marley's. I'm happy to read that the fish
lives next to Tokyo, in a place called Suruga Bay, where the
Pacific gets deep very fast. I page ahead. The second article is
on a tribe in Mali called the Dogon. Their shamans practice
divination by tracing a chart in the sand, baiting the chart
with peanuts, and reading it the following morning after a
desert fox has stepped in certain segments of it to nosh the
peanuts and offer advice. I'm charmed, I'm enchanted, I wish
I knew how to do that. I whisper to the glossy air, "I have to
tell Ben about this! How can you not eat mushrooms in a
world where fish have poison rainbows and foxes tell the
future?"*

But now, at the table in the co-op, when I tried to summon that shroomy delight, it wouldn't come. The lionfish didn't resemble Bob Marley anymore, and seemed to shrug. I stared up at the fried chicken stain again, that island-shaped instrument of seeing. I replayed the conversation I'd just had with Jennifer. I'd been all seriousness and heaviness; she, lightness, bubbliness, moist lips curving up in a smile that made me desperate to kiss her again. What if we were in a shipwreck and washed up on an island, just the two of us? Then she would, wouldn't she? Many times? My mind flicked back to the insanely sexy way we got together. We were planning a menu late at night, alone in the co-op, flirting and goofing off, and she ran to the fridge, ran back, and broke an egg on my head! So I—

"Horowitz, get your brain down off the wall a second." My good friend Mark Horwitz—presumably a distant cousin, he's from the Hungarian branch of the family, while I'm from the Polish—had stopped stroking the brown rodent of a goatee that clung to his chin, leaned over, and spoken to me. "See that guy over there?" Mark pointed to the stranger in the multicolored cap. "You should talk to him. His name's Jeremy Carver. You know how you're into the Amazon Jungle. He graduated two years ago and just got back from a year in South America."

"Cool." I scooped up four green peas on my spoon and catapulted them onto the table in front of the stranger, where they bounced and rolled. My contribution was noted but not reacted to. Soon, the conversation partners dispersed. I had an hour before my next class. I stood up cautiously—my lower back felt like a turkey fork was sunk in it, one prong on either side of the spine—and I went over and introduced myself to the visitor. "I'm interested in South America, especially the shamanism there, if you know anything about it," I said. "Could you tell me about your trip?"

"Sure thing," he said. "Have a seat." I eased myself onto a chair. One of the peas I had catapulted was in front of me. I ate it off the table with a twinge of remorse about wasting the other three, which were somewhere on the floor. Jeremy took a swig of black coffee and smoothed his sparse mustache with his fingertips. "I spent a lot of time in the jungle in Ecuador. I met some of the shamans. They're accepting outsiders as apprentices, 'cause the young people in the communities don't want to learn the old traditions anymore. And 'cause the missionaries are trying to stomp that stuff out. I got off a bus in a jungle town and met a shaman called Nenke from the Waorani tribe. The Waoranis are semi-wild. They've only had contact with outsiders for about thirty years. Nenke was waiting for me at the bus station. Said he knew I was coming."

"Huh."

"He walked with me into the forest and taught me about nature and the spirit world."

"Your Spanish must be really good."

"It isn't. His isn't either. It's hard to explain." The screen door banged. The co-op was emptying out. Wrapped in tefillin and a prayer shawl, an Orthodox guy swayed as he murmured his prayers by the window. Jeremy paused in the relative quiet to collect his thoughts. "Nenke taught me without speaking," he went on. "Telepathically. He told me every human has two spirit eyes in the chest midway between the nipples and the collarbones. You can use them to see energy. And spirits can come into you through the palm of your left hand and go out through the right. He was willing to keep teaching me, and I thought about accepting his offer. But I didn't want to live there."

"Why not?"

"I'm going into grad school in music. I play jazz saxophone. So when I went back to Quito after being with the Waoranis, I was at a youth hostel. This young shaman from another tribe called the Quichuas came to stay there. And that night, all night, I was in this half-dream, half-waking trance, where anacondas were attacking me. They were streaming toward me in the air. I couldn't stop them. Couldn't fight with them. Only thing I could do was dance with them. I redirected them away with my hands. Like this. They kept coming. I kept shifting them away. In the morning at breakfast, everyone in the hostel said they'd dreamed of getting attacked by anacondas. Later that day, the shaman admitted he'd tried to steal energy from everybody. Said his people had gotten pushed off their land. He was trying to gather energy to bring back and support them. It was a hunting expedition for power." Jeremy took another swig of coffee, looked at me to judge my reaction.

"No way," I said.

"Way," he said. "So since I've been back in the States, I keep dreaming of Waoranis. It feels

21

like the tribe is learning more about me by projecting themselves into my mind."

"Far out."

"One time when I was down there, I dreamed I was a jaguar running through the forest. I could sense everything like a jaguar does—the vision, the hearing, the smell, the taste in my mouth, the feel of my jaguar body, the weight of it, the power, the speed, the sensation of my paws whamming into the ground and springing forward off it."

"Did you try ayahuasca?" I released the question before it burned me. The stain on the wall was a spot on a jaguar's fur.

"I never tried it," Jeremy said. "It was around. I knew some people who did. I never needed it. I felt like I was tripping the whole time I was there. But some of the shamans drink it. And some of them share it with outsiders."

"Jeremy, what you've just told me is more interesting than anything I've heard in four and a half years of college."

He nodded and the multicolored tassels of his wool cap shook. "You should check out Ecuador, man."

4. Mother and Son

"Nobody would think you were weird if you went back to school, got married, and found a good job. You like literature and you're good at it. You could teach at a university."

I felt again that sensation like getting punched in the stomach. I wanted to yell at her, but I knew if I did, I'd start to cry. I spoke as evenly as I could: "I can't do that." I clenched my teeth and stuck my hands deeper into my jacket pockets.

The Newfoundland dog's claws clicked on the damp sidewalk to the rhythm of the sway of her midsection and hips. She looked strikingly like a modestly-sized black bear. She stopped to snuffle the base of a forsythia bush covered in tight green buds. We stopped too. From high in an elm tree, a songbird belted out a sharp melody. My mom would know the species' name. I didn't care. I wanted to get to the point where the bird could tell me its own name for itself.

I revisited something that had happened a week after I'd met Jeremy Carver. On a cold, bright autumn day, I smoked pot and sat on the worn, gray sandstone steps of Kosher Co-op. In the blue sky, *à la* Rimbaud, a white cloud looming over the campus took on the precise shape of the skeleton of a bottlenose dolphin grinning down at me with dozens of conical teeth. As clear as the apparition was, nobody else noticed it. Simultaneously—and with no apparent relationship between the two things—I became captivated by an idea that seemed more and more evident the more I thought about it.

The idea went like this. Around the time I was conceived, some shamans whose practices were threatened by missionary activity were conducting an ayahuasca ceremony, and as they lay in their hammocks in the darkness of a ceremonial hut, one or more of them sent out something—a wish, a prayer, an impulse, an atom of consciousness—that floated out through the world like a cool blue spark, traveling, wandering, until it met my inchoate soul, which was beginning to assemble itself, and which welcomed it in. The wish was that somebody born outside the forest would take up the work of the shamans, which was necessary to support life on Earth.

Apart from being a logical response by shamans to the threat to their practice, this explained why I'd always felt at odds with society and drawn to the wilderness.

But I knew I wouldn't be able to sell the story to my mom. And I knew, too, that it was likely to be just one of those things one thinks of while high on pot. I'd have to speak of acquiring valuable non-Western and pre-modern knowledge. As an academic, as an intellectual, she should accept that. But as usual, as soon as I opened my mouth, I deflated.

"I want to go to the jungle and study shamanism," I muttered, glancing at an oak tree for support. "The indigenous people know things that we've lost. About nature, and the spirit world, and healing."

24

"If they know so much about healing, why is the child mortality rate so high in the Third World?" she shot back. I couldn't answer. "And you're always talking about the spirit world. People want to believe in something because they're afraid of dying. In the Western world, we've been working since the Enlightenment to get rid of superstitions and see things the way they really are. You should read the Existentialists, as I keep telling you. Read Sartre and Camus. Then you wouldn't want to clutter up your head with crazy cosmologies from Cloud Cuckoo Land. That drug you told me the Indians take. Ayahooziedoozie or whatever it is. You want to know what tripping does to people? I'll take you to a mental hospital sometime and you can look at some of those people drooling in the back ward. Nathaniel, I spent far too much time and energy raising you to want to lose you to drugs."

"I don't think tripping can make someone crazy, just like that," I said. I didn't sound convinced. The thought crossed my mind again that I might be one of those people who shouldn't take psychedelics because they're already unstable.

My mom went on: "The other day I talked to a colleague of mine who researches brain chemistry at the university." We stopped at a corner to let a car go by. "Drugs like LSD damage people's genes. And *fry their brains*." She looked me in the eye, daring me to respond. Under her gray hair, her Irish eyes were unsmiling. The dog swung her own worried face around to glance at us, then turned back and sniffed the breeze blowing down the street. I couldn't think of anything to say.

25

Maybe my brain really was fried. I'd graduated a few months earlier, in December, and moved back in with my mom, my stepdad, and the dog in Ann Arbor. A month after that, I'd read a letter, wept, kicked a hole in my bedroom door, and mailed Jennifer a check for $370 to pay for an abortion, without knowing whether to believe her claim that she'd been pregnant.

Maybe it was my heart that was fried.

We crossed the street in silence and entered the park. The gray sky sagged like a dirty sheet. A three-story brick box with windows came into view: my elementary school. I heard a sad clank I remembered from childhood: the breeze banging the aluminum pulley against the aluminum flagpole, as it had, day and night, for decades. I wished my mom would walk home alone so I could let the dog off the leash and climb the hill.

"I'll tell you what," she said, conciliatory. "I think there might be things you could talk about with a therapist. If you want, I'll call around and make an appointment for you. If you find someone you like, you can work with them."

I considered this. At least it would get her off my back for a while. And it would be good to unload my problems on someone. As I opened my mouth to accept, a coughing fit doubled me over. When I straightened up, her furious eyes pierced me. "Are you smoking dope again?"

Yes, I would have a lot to talk about with the therapist.

5. The Talking Cure

"The irony about my mom not believing in psychic experiences is that she had a really strong one the night her brother died. I had a hockey coach who always reminded her of him. So she has this dream that my coach is dying on an operating table. Doctors are trying to save his life. It's not working. She's crying *really hard*. And she wakes up with the sound of a crash echoing in her ears. She looks at the digital clock on the bedside table: 4:17 a.m. She goes back to sleep. Two hours later, phone rings. It's her sister Anne, sobbing, 'Pat's dead! Pat's dead!' He'd been out late at a union meeting, had a few beers. On the way home he totaled his car and his body. He died on the operating table at exactly 4:17. Am I crazy to think that's interesting?"

Doctor Seligmann raised his black eyebrows. "No." His Brooklyn accent was audible even in that one syllable. His interlaced fingers rested on the belly of his multicolored sweater as he waited for me to proceed. In his early 50s, he was trim and sporty, with a ready smile.

"I don't want to go straight to the Amazon," I told Seligmann. "I want to go to Mexico first, check out peyote and Mexican shamanism, and get fluent in Spanish. Then head down to Ecuador and study with a shaman who drinks ayahuasca."

That was my plan, such as it was. I was secretly scared I'd blurt out twisted sexual fantasies on these hallucinogens, or go permanently insane, as my mom warned. But I was more scared of doing nothing.

I went on, "Maybe I could be healed that way. And maybe help other people too."

I secretly hoped the Indians would recognize my aptitude for magic and make me their leader, and we'd

27

fight a guerrilla war against deforestation, oil companies, and the desacralization of nature.

I had my literary dream, too.

I said, "I want to take notes in a journal, then write a book. In Joyce's *Ulysses*, ordinary people's lives become mythic and profound because of how he writes about them. So the *material* isn't so important. What's important is how you *treat* the material." Seligmann appeared to be paying attention, so I went on. "I mean, I know I'm no James Joyce." Secretly, I thought I *was* a James Joyce. I changed tack, confused. "We did this exercise in my writing classes where we went to a place and sat down and wrote everything that was going on, everything we saw and heard and smelled and felt. It was like my dad sitting down and sketching the scenery around him. I could do that in the jungle. It would pick up information you couldn't get through any other medium."

Seligmann said, "A word is worth a thousand pictures, eh?"

"Ha. Yeah. And, by telling *my* story, I want to tell *everyone's* story. They told us in writing class: the more specific, the more universal. 'Cause we all experience love, fear, pain, joy, death, all that stuff. And then if you could bring that specificity, which is universal, to material that's really far outside the mainstream of Western lit—like shamanism—you'd end up with something really new."

Seligmann waited for me to continue, but I looked away, imagining reviews. "Brilliant. Visionary. Astounding." "Kerouac meets Castaneda in the rainforest." "Gonzo mythology—Joseph Campbell and Carl Jung trip with Hunter S. Thompson." "The author is enchanted by every speck of dirt and every puff of wind, convinced it contains a lesson … no flight of fancy is too trivial to record."

***

"Every time I meet a woman I go through this whole cycle of 'You're so beautiful, you're the most beautiful woman I've ever seen, I could love you for the rest of my life.' And then we get involved, and after a while it doesn't work, because I have no idea how to be in a romantic relationship, but I stay in it because we're having sex. My body becomes addicted to having orgasms with her. Every time I'm around her that's all I want to do—instead of, like, *talking*, or walking around. We end up hating each other and she breaks up with me, and a month later I meet another woman and it starts up again."

"That sounds pretty bleak. Is it really that bad all the time?"

"No. It's amazing, too. We learn from each other, and from being together." I nibbled my lower lip, remembering nibbling other lower lips. "I have this idea that I should try out as many women as I can, and if there's one of them who I still have something to talk about with after we've had sex a bunch of times, that's who I should marry. See, I think my parents got married too early, before either of them had played around enough, and that caused problems in their marriage. I don't want to make that mistake. And that's why I don't stay single for long. There's usually someone else nice around," I concluded.

"You remind me of something I saw last winter," Seligmann said. "First big snow we had, I went over to a friend's house and we walked his dog. The dog was less than a year old and he'd never been in snow before. And when he got out in the snow, he wanted to jump in all of it! He went galloping around and leaping into the snow and biting it. He'd see some more snow over there and

29

jump in it, and then see some more over there. You could see him thinking, *Wow! Yes!* and he'd jump in that too."

***

"Jeremy Carver reminded me of a dream I had when I was fifteen. There's another dream I want to talk about, but let me get to that in a minute. So a nuclear war wipes out almost all of humanity. I'm walking through the wrecked streets of an American city. I see the dead body of a drug dealer I know, lying across the sidewalk. I go through the pockets of his jeans. I find a light blue pill. Mescaline. I swallow the pill and keep walking. Two jaguars walk out of a deserted store and come toward me, a male and a female, brother and sister. They tell me telepathically to have sex with the female! I'm like, 'What? No way!' They rush me and claw my thighs, letting me know they'll kill me if I don't. So I follow them inside the store. Then I wake up. I don't know what it means."

"What are your early associations with wild cats?"

"I played the Cowardly Lion in *The Wizard of Oz* at my kindergarten. The role was perfect for me. I was big but I was always getting beaten up by other kids. Anybody who wanted could come up and take a swing at me. I'd get weak. I couldn't fight back. But the lion goes off searching for the wizard who can give him courage, and at the end of the play I drank a bottle of red pop and got my courage and roared. My mom made me a lion costume out of orange-brown felt. I kept it in my closet for years."

"Sounds like you were a closet lion. No wonder the jaguar lady wanted you. What's the other dream?"

"This one's really fucked up. I dreamed I was writing down ideas for poems. I blacked out for a little while, and when I came to, there was another line written in the notebook in different handwriting. It said, 'I'm inside you now.' I woke up in this crazy panic, afraid I was going to hurt someone."

"And what does that say to you?"

"That there's some outside energy in me that I've got to get out before I really do hurt someone."

"You believe that?"

"I don't disbelieve it."

"Without wanting to deny the validity of what you're saying, I'd caution you against giving too much authority to a single image from a dream. People dream about all kinds of things, some of them pretty scary."

"OK, so, tamp it down, maybe give me some medication, and count the months before I end up in jail or a mental institution, or dead." I glared at Dr. Seligmann, who regarded me calmly, then smiled.

"You know, you looked almost like a warrior when you said that. You looked like you were about ready to take up arms and fight against whatever it is that's bothering you. You keep telling me you want to study shamanism. In the seven weeks you've been coming here, I haven't thought of a single good reason why you shouldn't. If that's something you really feel you need to do, don't waste any more time around here."

6. How the Sun Turned Blue and Exploded

Soon after Seligmann gave me the green light, an Aztec shaman materialized in my home town. Nezahualcoyotl was from Mexico City and had been invited to speak at a university seminar on mysticism hosted by the Religion Department. In his 70s, he was pudgy, and short even for a Mexican, with umber skin, a salt-and-pepper goatee, a melodious voice, and eyes like interstellar voids. In the months and years to come, I would refer back to his speech as I sought to understand what was happening to me.

The chair of the department said, "Nezahualcoyotl and his students were the first Mexicans to participate in the sun dance of the Lakota Sioux in North Dakota, and he was later given permission to put on sun dances of his own. His name means 'Fasting Coyote' in Nahuatl, the language of the Aztecs. The original bearer of the name was a king in pre-Columbian Mexico.

"The sun dance was banned for decades by the US government as pagan and seditious, then legalized in the 1970s. For four days, the people fast from food and water, and dance in a circle around a tree representing the axis of the world. They dedicate their energy and their suffering to the sun, to thank the Great Spirit for warming and illuminating the world. Some choose to undergo a further sacrifice, allowing their chests to be pierced and themselves to be hoisted up off the ground to hang by the piercings. From what I understand, Nezahualcoyotl is going to tell us a little about that."

Through an interpreter, the old man began to speak. "I find that the mystical thing is a bit beyond the religious," he said. "It's beyond personal achievement, or other people. The mystical state is a feeling.

32

"Perhaps I don't consider myself very mystical, but I fall under many definitions of the mystic." He pushed his fingers through his goatee as if combing out thoughts his ancestors had planted in their own sparse beards.

"Why do I dedicate myself to that? Why do I investigate? Why do I have my experiences? Because inside me, I have my message. At the moment of conception, we receive cosmic energies. They come to where the conception is taking place. These energies are sent from every point in the universe. We're mixes of energies, codes of energies that mix together inside us. And each of us has a mission: to preserve the chain of evolution and to enrich it with our own experiences. The system is always forming different beings because the components that make it up are always in flux. The earth is always moving around the sun; the sun is moving, too. So it's impossible for two people to be exactly the same.

"In every generation, a certain number are born who are different from the rest. It's not that they're superior to the others. Nothing draws your attention. They live in their own worlds. They don't begin to talk at an early age. Or maybe they don't pronounce words well. Sometimes they talk confusedly, or in a loud voice, or so softly you can hardly hear. They live in a different world. They're mystics, people who are outside this world without being outside it. They like to be alone. They find places where the energies appear. There, they feel very calm, and they have their experiences. They don't look for places of power: their destiny takes them there. They don't look for experiences: they receive them. They have access to visions, to revelations, of things that can't be perceived by everyone. Sometimes they seem to hear voices. They say, 'Ah! Someone's communicating with me.' Also, they begin to feel sensations in their body. They feel like hands are stroking them when the wind blows. Or they feel the caresses of the sun. It's not an idea, not a theory, it's really energy from the sun: not only light and heat, but many other kinds too. They don't know why, but sometimes it makes them want to cry. Why does this happen? Because they're sensitive. And they're following a process of further sensitization. At first, they might feel bad. They don't know what's happening. But they get used to receiving these messages, which become clearer and clearer. And they begin to experiment, little by little, little by little. When a communication takes place, they say, 'Welcome. I want more.'

"And so it happens that they have no more fear of death. They're not afraid of spirits or ghosts, either. They're not afraid of the unknown. They seek it out. They perceive another world. And the other world is what's beyond death. So death is nothing to them. After their body breaks down, they continue to exist. So this world isn't so important anymore. It's the other world that attracts them, and where they're certain to be happy. They're here because, physically, they've been put here. But with other senses beyond the five physical ones, they perceive the other world, and they can travel within it.

"The ceremonies, and the whole indigenous world that we're developing, are different from the Western world. Our values are different. We're not enslaved by money. We attract it, it comes, we spend it.

"And we welcome all the perceptions that come to us.

"When we lose our fear of death, and of the unknown, we start to really live. At least, speaking for myself, I've reached the conclusion that the world we're living in right now isn't real. It's a lie. It's only a form in our mind. Our senses perceive it because they're conditioned to perceive this universe, which is an energy that's vibrating at a special frequency. This universe doesn't exist at other wavelengths.

"Right now, right here, there are millions of radio waves. They're being transmitted by thousands of stations all over the world. We can turn on a radio and bring them in. The radio contains crystals which, if they approach one another, vibrate a certain number of times per second. And if they draw apart, they vibrate at another number of times per second. For example, nine hundred kilocycles, and you have a whole world of sound, of messages, of music. You move the crystals and you have another. This reminds us that we're vibrating at a wavelength which permits the existence of this moment, and this space, but which has no validity in others. And there are innumerable waves. Radio waves, television waves, cosmic waves, an infinite number. So you become aware that this world isn't so much, that it's not so valuable. The important thing is the experiences you have.

"A person who decides to be a mystic can become one. But it's going to cost a lot of suffering. We call it the path of pain. You have to suffer to dominate your appetites. You follow special diets. You close yourself off to the pleasures and satisfactions of this world. You work on this from sunrise to sunset every day of your life."

Pausing, he ran his fingers through his beard again.

"The mission of the mystic isn't to be world-famous. It's not to gain power or a lot of money. It's not to stand out. It's simply to examine all the sensations that come. And each one of them leads closer to ecstasy, which is the goal of the mystic. How do we define ecstasy? It's a marvelous state. You feel you become weightless. You lose all feelings of pain and fear. You find yourself floating far above them.

"I want to bring myself to the state of ecstasy. It's somewhat like orgasm. But an orgasm lasts only some

35

seconds. With mysticism, the ecstasy goes for hours. It's a beautiful thing to hold onto this vibration. It's the greatest sensation that it's possible to achieve.

"But it's not something that happens by accident. You go out in nature. You feel something sweet in your mouth. Later, you feel warm. Time doesn't exist. There's nothing but light. It's not a light that blinds you. It's a light that embraces you, that gathers you in. An energy soft as velvet. In these moments, you perceive another way of life, another reality. You can see the universe in its totality. Even more, you can *understand* it. You can open your arms and embrace everything.

"You're in communication with something superior. And if you ask it, 'Does the universe have an end?', it says 'Yes.'

"At least, that's what it said to me.

"I said, '*Where* does the universe end?'

"It said, 'Where time is frozen, where time is congealed, that's where this universe has its end.'

"Once I was at a sun dance," Nezahualcoyotl went on. "Hanging from the tree. Suffering like mad. Twisting around. They cut into your chest and put in pegs attached to ropes. They haul you up by the skin of your chest so you're hanging from the tree. You feel your chest slowly ripping. You feel your blood dripping from the wounds. You feel unimaginable pain. It goes up to your head. Like your brain is on fire. You see everything in red. But you tolerate the pain, because it's your sacrifice, and you want to feel it.

"I was hanging there in the most absolute agony. I was spinning. But I was also holding eagle wings, one in each hand. I stretched out my arms, and with the wings, I stabilized myself in the air, like an eagle flying.

"Then I looked right at the sun.

"In that moment, the sun turned blue.

36

"The pain was gone. The sensation of hanging by the skin of my chest was gone. I felt I was flying like an eagle. I entered ecstasy. And I saw the blue sun explode. *Pshhhh!* An enormous explosion.

"Something said to me that the whole universe had exploded. I saw it expanding in a sphere, at a tremendous velocity. I was in the middle, at the axis. Later, it slowed down, little by little, little by little, until it stopped. Then it converted into energy, into light.

"A voice said to me, 'What you're seeing is all the matter that exists in the universe. It's focusing itself again.'

"I watched it, feeling this beautiful vibration. The light resolved into the shape of an enormous ring balancing in space. It shone like it was made of diamonds, and the diamonds were suns, sparkling—millions and billions of suns glittering in this enormous ring of energy.

"The voice said to me, 'This is your name.'

"At that moment, the ecstasy left me. I felt myself falling. Suddenly I was on all fours on the ground. My skin had broken through. I'd fallen from very high up in the tree. Friends helped me stand up.

"That was a mystical experience. It showed me the path. It supports me to this day. Now I can enter this state of ecstasy any time I want. I can feel the sensation, and it may last minutes or hours, as long as I want, wherever I am. Riding on a plane, on a bus, when I'm eating, when I'm sleeping, when I'm taking a shower, whenever I want. It's like a prize. For me, that's mysticism. It's an experience that guided me to itself. And I can be infinitely happy whenever I want.

"Perhaps I can't make a scientific analysis of mysticism. But what I've said is my own experience. Consider it, then, as something personal. Thank you. Aho."

During the question and answer session, he said he was holding a sun dance in Mexico in two months. He invited anyone in the audience to attend if they happened to be in the area. I decided to happen to be in the area.

7. Where Anglos Fear to Tread

I flew to Mexico City and bussed to Guadalajara. I had the number of someone who knew where the ceremony was going to be. I phoned from my hotel. The connection was bad. My Spanish was worse. The man kept squawking, "Ah hee heek." He sounded like a huge bird.

I said, "*¿Qué?*"

I imagined him flapping big black wings twice before he repeated, "Ah hee heek. *Ah hee heek.*"

Finally, he spelled it for me. I wrote it down: *ah, hota, eee, hota, eee, say*: A-J-I-J-I-C.

Next day at sunset, I reached the base of a high, rocky hill in the town of Ajijic. I walked up a steep, dusty trail, breathing the smell of pines, thrilled to be on ground consecrated for indigenous ceremonies. *Ah hee heek,* I murmured, greeting the place.

At the top, a few dozen people bustled around in the twilight among tents and cooking fires. A Mexican guy a few years younger than me asked if I needed food or a place to sleep. I said yes to both, and he and his two younger brothers immediately found me a hot meal and a tipi with some free space in it. They pointed out a contingent of new age gringos from Pennsylvania, but when I met them, I learned those gringos had been studying with Nezahualcoyotl for several years and wanted nothing to do with an outsider, a novice. The four-day ceremony would begin the following morning.

The day dawned cool and overcast. The dance ground was a round, flat space with a tree in the middle. Stately Nezahualcoyotl and a score of dancers appeared from where they'd camped nearby. The men wore white loincloths, the women white dresses. The mystic blew a

39

long, clear note on a conch shell and began to speak, a Pennsylvanian translating his words into English. "Brothers and sisters from far and near, welcome to this sacred ceremony. To begin, I'm going to say a few words to clarify our traditional beliefs, our traditional understandings. Five hundred years ago, the chroniclers of the Spanish invasions wrote of the primitive religion of the primitive people they had come to subjugate. In their writings, they justified their actions. In their writings, they spoke of Aztec 'gods.' That was an intellectual mistake. The chroniclers imported a European concept to a context in which it did not apply. Quetzalcoatl, Tezcatlipoca, Tlaloc, Coatlique, Huizilopochtli, all those so-called gods were considered by the Aztec people to be *symbols* of the divine, expressing its visible facets, its apprehensible characteristics.

"For our ancestors, animals, similarly, symbolized truths about the universe. The snake, for instance, because it's always in contact with the ground, represented the wisdom of the earth. Only Christianity demonized it. So when the indigenous person honored the serpent, when he meditated on the serpent in order to understand and love the earth, the Spanish said he was worshipping the Devil. Nothing could be further from the truth. It was the Spanish who brought the Devil here from across the sea.

"An Aztec teacher," Nezahualcoyotl went on, "would say to his students: 'What does the divine seem like to you?' One would say, 'Like a feathered serpent, combining the wisdom of the earth and sky, spreading intelligence across the cosmos.' 'Yes,' the teacher would say, 'you're right. And you, how does the divine seem to you?' Another student would say, 'Like the moon. We don't always see it, but it is cool and clear and beautiful, and it can give us light when we need to travel in the darkness.' The teacher would say, 'You're absolutely right

40

too. And you?' A third student would say, 'To me, the divine seems most like the sun, because the sun shines on everyone and gives life to everything—to the brothers and sisters who walk on two legs, to those who walk on four legs, those who fly, those who creep, those who swim, to all the plants, and even to all the minerals on earth.' 'You're right, too,' the teacher would say. 'Everything you've all said is correct.'

"Now, my friends, my family, it's the sun, that visible, tactile facet of the divine, for which we dance today, in gratitude for the countless forms of solar energy that reveal the world to our eyes, that warm us, that nourish life on our Mother Earth, from the tiniest microbes to the greatest trees of the greatest forests. Aho!"

Under his ocelot-fur headband, his eyes scanned the horizon or beyond. He blew another note on his conch shell. At that very moment, the clouds cracked open and sunlight spilled across the hilltop. And the dancers entered the circle.

For most of the day they danced in place or trotted around the tree to the beat of the *huehuetl*, a standing drum made from a hollowed-out tree trunk with a skin across the top. The light and heat became intense. Four times the dancers paused and went into a big tent to smoke tobacco in pipes made of wood and stone for twenty minutes before resuming the dance.

The second day was like the first.

On the third morning, one of the dancers made a flesh sacrifice. It wasn't as intense as the one Nezahualcoyotl had described. Another man pierced the skin over the sacrificer's pectoral muscles and inserted wooden pegs that were attached to a rope that went over the tree and were tied to a log on the other side. Two men picked up the log and ran with it so the pegs burst out of

41

the dancer's chest. An older dancer administered a red powder to the two wounds.

This was repeated by other dancers that day and the next.

I didn't know it at the time, but someone I would meet later was alone in a cave elsewhere in the hill, eating peyote and meditating.

The spectators relaxed and talked with each other. We went to the edges of the hilltop and ate bread and cheese and looked out at hills, valleys, towns, railways, highways, vultures, songbirds, clouds.

A worrisome note was that, due to the hot, dry weather, and the scarcity of water that had to be hauled from a spring, and the shortage of fruit, I never quite needed to walk the long trail that led to the outhouse.

I learned that Nezahualcoyotl had a kind of nemesis, a younger shaman named Carlos Cuitláhuac. This Cuitláhuac had stolen Nezahualcoyotl's project to commemorate the 500th anniversary of Christopher Columbus's arrival in the Americas with the Journeys for Peace and Dignity, a dual-start relay run to be performed by indigenous people leaving simultaneously from the northern coast of Alaska and the southern tip of Chile and meeting at the pyramids of Teotihuacan near Mexico City on October 12, 1992. Some Machiavellian maneuvering had given Cuitláhuac control over the Journeys.

Asking around about this movement to promote pre-Columbian traditions that had been hidden since the conquest, I received a photocopy of a text, which I translate below. It's about the moment when a so-called paganism—whatever that might mean—went underground. México-Tenochtitlan is now Mexico City. Anahuac is the Aztec Empire, and Nahuatl is, again, the language of the Aztecs. The text purports to be the last speech by their last leader before the empire fell to the Spaniards.

Last decree of Cuauhtémoc, lord of México-Tenochtitlan
15 August, 1521
(Nahuatl oral tradition)

Our sun has been eclipsed,
our sun has been hidden away,
and it has left us in the most complete darkness.
We know it will rise again to illuminate us once
more;
but while it stays down there in the land of the
dead,
we have to join together and hide within our hearts
everything we love.
We have to destroy our *teokaltin*, our temples;
our *kalmekameh*, schools of advanced studies;
our *tlachkouan*, ball courts;
our *telpochkaltin*, schools for children;
and our *kuikakaltin*, song houses.
We have to leave the streets empty,
and shut ourselves in our homes.
From now on, our homes will be our teokaltin,
our kalmekameh,
our tlachkouan,
our telpochkaltin,
and our kuikakaltin.
From now on, until the new sun rises,
the fathers and the mothers will be the teachers and
the guides,
and they will take their children's hands
and they will walk beside them
as long as they live.

43

May the fathers and mothers not forget to tell their
children
    what Anahuac was—
    under the protection of our gods,
    and as a result of the customs and the education
    that our elders passed down to our parents,
    and that they, with so much determination,
    passed down to us.
    May they not forget, either, to tell their children
    of what, one day, Anahuac again will be.

***

"So did they have gods or not? It says gods here," I
said to the guy who gave me the text. "*Dioses.*"

"Maybe the Nahuatl is mistranslated," he said.
"Maybe it should be *fuerzas divinas,* divine forces."

"What about human sacrifice?" I asked. "The
Aztecs were famous for it, no?"

"Yeah. Nezahualcoyotl says it didn't happen. Says it
was all made up by the Spaniards. I don't think that's right.
But, in any case, what the Spaniards did was much worse."

***

After the sun dance was over, the three brothers
loaded me into a sky-blue Volkswagen Beetle and drove
me to their home in Guadalajara. This was a compound of
two one-story houses at either end of a courtyard,
surrounded by a brick wall topped with broken glass. The
boys' mom and sister both worked as nurses. They made
me feel right at home, lodging me with the boys in a room
in the house at the back of the compound. Two cousins
were visiting, staying in the front house where the kitchen
and the bathroom were—curvaceous bleach blonde

44

newlywed nineteen and doe-eyed budding first onslaught of puberty.

"You gotta watch out for Campeón," said the oldest brother. "By the wall there. He's an Akita. Guards the compound. My brothers and I have scars on our arms from him. The German shepherd, we adopted last week. She doesn't have a name yet. We just call her Novia 'cause she's his girlfriend."

The word "girlfriend" flashed through my mind again when I met the daughter of the family, tall, slender, named after an Aztec princess. She and her mom showed me how to wash my clothes by hand in the outdoor wash basin. As I scrubbed soap suds and dirt in a gym sock heel against the rough cement, the women laughed at my awkwardness. I said, "In my country, we have machines that do this."

The mom pointed at the daughter. "This is my machine!" The two of them cackled.

At dusk, we feasted on a food of old Anahuac, homemade tamales, corn cakes steamed in corn husks: savory ones filled with spicy pork, mild chicken and vegetables, or hot poblano chili with cinnamon; sweet ones packing strawberry, pineapple, coconut, quince jelly, or candied cactus. My mouth was in heaven.

I pondered this trip. Entering Mexico, I'd felt an immediate alleviation of my stress. Evidently the pattern of energy that oppressed me was mostly specific to the USA. My social awkwardness had dropped away. Whatever I did, people figured it wasn't because I was weird, but because I was a foreigner. And they appreciated that I'd left the glorious, comfortable, wealthy North for a solo journey through the unsafe, impoverished South. I resolved to return to Mexico as soon as I'd saved more money.

At two a.m., my large intestine punched me awake. "Dude," it grumbled, "you haven't shat in five days."

"Talk to me about it in the morning, asshole," I said.

"No, you have to go now," it said.

"You've held out this long. You can wait till morning."

"I repeat," my bowel insisted, *you must go now.*

"Fuck you! Morning!"

"GET UP NOW," it roared, punching and kicking.

"OK, OK."

The toilet was in the other house. I sat up and hatched a desperate plan. It seemed impossible, but it was my only hope. I would tiptoe across the patio past the sleeping guard dogs, ease open the creaky metal door, slide like a tendril of mist through the kitchen disturbing no pot-pan-silverware-dish, creep past the two sleeping girls, slink behind the curtain, evacuate a five-day backlog of ex-food in sepulchral silence, flush it all down using the red plastic bucket that was kept on the floor next to the blue plastic barrel that was always full of water for bathing and flushing the toilet, then return to where I was now.

In jockey shorts, trembling, punched from within, I set out on this quest-within-a-quest. *Is this what Nezahualcoyotl meant by the mystic's path of pain?* I wondered, stepping on a sharp stone. *What if I lose my shit right here in the middle of the patio? Must keep the sphincter clenched! Strong!*

Claws clicking cement, a dark shape hurled toward me out of the darkness. It snarled like Cerberus and bared its slavering fangs at the potential future generations of my family.

I froze.

Campeón froze too.

I edged forward.

46

This Japanese demon of the Mexican underworld seethed with fury, bass notes of rage rumbling in his throat.

I froze again.

His girlfriend admired him from the shadows.

I telepathed, "Please?"

Bass notes rumbled.

I telepathed, "I'm sorry about this, but I really have to use the bathroom."

He growled louder. *Farewell, balls,* I thought. *It's been good.*

But, finally, bored, Campeón let me inch past him. *Awesome, brother. Thank you.*

I ninjaed inside, and, miraculously, did all my business without waking the girls. *I'm a superhero. A thousand pounds lighter. Gonna waltz back across this patio. Campeón's my friend. Warm bed and dreamland, I'm coming home.*

But, Novia beside him now, the Akita blocked me again. And snarled to let me know he was serious. And then that bastard mounted his girlfriend. Growling murderously every time I made a move, he proceeded to fuck her silly, both of them watching me with big assholic grins on their doggy faces.

Finally, they got their rocks off and let me take mine safely to bed.

***

When I got back to Ann Arbor, I found one cycle of family life had ended and another begun: after a nineteen-year marriage, my stepdad Walt had moved out of the house and filed for divorce. My family was smashed again. At first, I was enraged at Walt, but then I didn't blame him. He and my mom hadn't been getting along for years.

47

I kept living rent-free in the basement of the heavily mortgaged house that was hers now. She took in borders to make ends meet. I landed a job as the invoice clerk of the textbook department of a university bookstore. A 9-to-5 desk job, just what I'd wanted to avoid, but I knew I wouldn't get trapped in it, as I wasn't staying long: I planned to stay exactly a year and then head back to Mexico, then on down to Ecuador. On my first day, my supervisor took me around to meet my co-workers. In charge of medical reference books was Lily, a stunningly attractive, aloof Thai woman in her early 30s. Standing at a filing cabinet, she barely looked up when we were introduced. My mind performed the spontaneous arithmetic of subtracting her clothes and the bookstore and adding a jungle scene. The filing cabinet became a waterfall. Passion flowers and morpho butterflies bobbed in the breeze, and Lily was naked of everything but splendor. Over the next months, I learned she was fed up with her marriage to a former US marine. Filled with shame and joy, we started a lunchtime love affair in public spaces downtown where two panting bodies could be concealed—the bell tower, the inside corner of the brick wall around the abandoned fraternity that couldn't be seen from the street, the roof of the building where we worked. Four months after that, she left her husband and teenage son and moved in with my mom and me, *bam*, just like that. My mom said it would be fine as long as she paid rent.

Half of me was convinced Lily was the one I was going to spend my life with. This conviction came naturally whenever I fell in love. My cynical side argued that I was using her as a placeholder for someone I might be in a steady relationship with in the future, while she was using me as a stepping stone to get out of her marriage. I hated the lack of self-control that had brought me into the relationship. But I loved holding her.

I had one confrontation with her husband. He blamed her for what had happened, but he told me, "You have no morals." The words stung, though I reminded myself that in other areas of my life I did indeed have morals. I tried to use as little plastic as possible, I'd canvassed for Greenpeace during summers in Ann Arbor, Seattle, and Los Angeles, I voted Democratic, I didn't eat much meat or use excessive detergent on my clothes, et cetera.

But yeah, I reflected, *it would be good if I could find a moral compass inside myself. Learn the difference between right and wrong and stick to it. Because the way I am right now, I just don't know.*

One day I became convinced hubby might take a pistol and shoot me in the head. I'd see a flash of light and the sidewalk spinning up at me and that would be it. *If I had more control over my sex drive,* I thought, *I wouldn't be at risk of getting murdered by jealous husbands. But I don't, so I am.*

When I flew to Mexico to begin my next journey in October, 1992, Lily flew with me. We went to the pyramids of Teotihuacan and caught the end of the Journeys for Peace and Dignity, though we saw neither stately Nezahualcoyotl nor the sinister Cuitláhuac. Next we went to Cancun to snorkel and make love. Then it was time for her to go back to her job and finalize her divorce, and for me to investigate indigenous worldviews around Mexico and take an exploratory trip to Ecuador. We'd keep in touch by phone when possible.

When Lily's plane lifted off at dawn, I sat on the floor of the airport leaning against a column for a quarter of an hour, tears dripping into my Madras plaid shirt. My life was over. I dragged my sorry ass up, went back to the hotel, cried more, showered, lay on the balcony watching

49

high white clouds and trying to decide what they looked like, packed my backpack, checked out, and headed off to the bus station, where I bought a ticket to Puebla, the nearest city to a village in the mountains of central Mexico where Nezahualcoyotl was putting on a four-night moon dance ceremony.

On the bus, a friendly Mexican sat next to me. I was glad to have Aníbal's company so I wouldn't be stuck inside my head missing Lily for the eighteen-hour trip. He was missing his left hand. Bandits cut it off, he said. He had a special watch on the stump. "Look," he said, and pressed a button and ignited a flame: it was a lighter. He lived in Puebla. He'd been in Cancun for a month looking for work. He hadn't found any, and he'd had to sell a gold necklace for cash to buy food. But he was optimistic that things would improve.

The bus stopped for lunch at a restaurant. We all filed off. Aníbal asked me to buy him lunch because he had no money. "OK," I said. *So that's what this is about.*

We talked straight on through. A few hours later the bus stopped again and I bought us dinner.

At 10:30 p.m. we were approaching Puebla, a city I didn't know. "Hey, Aníbal, can you put me up for the night at your place?"

"Oh, no," he said.

"Why not?"

"You wouldn't like it."

"Why wouldn't I?"

"It's really dirty."

"I don't care."

"The electricity got turned off because I didn't pay it."

"I just need a place to sleep. If it's good enough for you, it's good enough for me."

50

"My friends were in there sniffing *thinner* while I was gone." He used the English word, pronouncing it "teen air."

"So?"

"Oh, no. Really."

"Oh, yes, really. I bought you lunch. I bought you dinner. Now you can help me too." He shook his head and then finally nodded.

From the bus station, we walked half an hour. Our first stop was a restaurant that sold cheap tacos made from the heads of cows. He ordered four with brain, I four with cheek. I doused mine in a respectable, homemade hot sauce that contained cilantro. The cheek was tough and chewy, but easier to—if you'll pardon the expression—wrap my head around, than brain, tongue, or eyeball would have been.

Then Aníbal brought me into a bar. Not to drink, he explained, but so we could empty our bladders. The regulars and the bartender knew him and welcomed him home. Finally, we came to a block of what looked like storage units. Because it was on a corner, his unit had a tiny window. A light rain was falling. The padlock on the metal door was stuck: he couldn't twist the key in it. Though it was late, there was activity in the next unit. "Borrow some vegetable oil from your neighbor," I said. He did. The lock opened.

The smell hit us as we went in, fermented mash of dirty clothes and paint thinner. Evidently, his friends had left the jug open. Where was it? By the light from the doorway he searched for it, then knocked it over. It sloshed on the floor. He mopped up the liquid and capped the jug. Peace returned. The rain pattered gently on the zinc roof. Aníbal located a candle and lit it with his watch, then closed and bolted the door.

He bedded down on a mat on the floor, I on a soft fold-out chair. At four I woke needing to piss. A rat scampered out through the crack under the door. Aníbal woke too, saying, "You need to piss?" He led me outside and indicated a square hole in the cement pavement with water in it, then disappeared around a corner. I started to piss in the hole. He came back around the corner, hissing, "No! That's the water people use for washing clothes."

I braked in mid-stream, having increased the squalidity of these squalid lives. Nothing to do about it now. I followed Aníbal around the corner to an open space and finished there.

In the morning, he hit me up for another ten bucks and I went back to the bus station and traveled to the village where the moon dance was. I felt better when I got there. There was nature, there was venison, there were spiritual people.

By day, everyone who wasn't a dancer tended to go in sweatlodges and sing Nahuatl songs to the beat of a frame drum. By night, nine women in long white dresses danced within a circle whose perimeter was delineated with four fires oriented to the four directions. Because of my origin, I was put in charge of caring for the fire of the North, and spent long, quiet hours next to it, feeding it wood. A local boy kept me company, quizzing me about my homeland and repeating words and phrases in English.

After the ceremony, I stayed in the village. I got to know Jamie Bear. Round glasses. Long salt-and-pepper ponytail. He was the only other English speaker, and relied on me to interpret for him. Said he'd relocated to Mexico because he was on the run from the FBI for destroying property while protesting coal mining in Arizona at a place called Black Mesa. He was half Arizona Indian and half Alaska Indian, and a veteran of the 1973 Wounded Knee

52

uprising, when members of the American Indian Movement battled the US Army for 71 days.

He was a pipe carrier, authorized to possess a *chanupa* of the Lakota people, the wood and stone pipe that the sun dancers had smoked in Ajijic. He'd bring it out out every morning at dawn with a few villagers and me. We'd face Iztaccíhuatl, the snow-capped volcano that dominated the landscape beyond the evergreen forest. In the cold, pine-scented breeze, far from the noise of any machine, the Native American outlaw would pack and light the chanupa, puff on it, and say, *Thank you, Tunkashila, Great Spirit, for letting me live to see this day. Thank you for my life, for this moment, for my health, for this village, for the good people around me. Thank you for the earth and the sun that give us what we need to live. For the nature all around us, and all our relations, the four-legged people, the two-legged people, the ones who crawl, the ones who fly; the animals that give us their meat and their milk; the plants that drink in the light of the sun and give us their bodies. Tunkashila, please bless them all. And bless the humans, here and all over the world. Many of your children are sick today. Please help them find healing. Many of them are hungry. Please help them find food. Many of them are in prison. Please help them find freedom. Thank you, Tunkashila. Ho.*

Then he'd pass the pipe to us, share its fragrant, bitter smoke.

Over dinner, Jamie told me he'd been in peyote ceremonies in the Native American Church, together with Lakota medicine man Leonard Crow Dog. "The tipi was the world's first spaceship," Jamie said. "You can go anywhere in the universe with it." The round windows of his glasses reflected candle flames and darkness.

"I've decided to try to study to be a shaman," I said. "That's what I'm doing here in Latin America."

"Here's what Uncle Leonard told me you have to pray if you want to be a healer, a medicine man: 'Great

53

Spirit, please grant me a vision and the power to heal.' But you gotta be careful if you do that. You gotta have total respect for the sacred. You can't play around with it."

"I understand. I'll try to be respectful."

"One time I wasn't respectful. I paid for it. Real bad."

"What happened?"

"Smoked a joint laced with angel dust. PCP. Got all fucked up. Picked up my eagle-feather peyote fan and started playin' around with it. Couple days later I called Uncle Leonard on the phone. He picked up. Before I had a chance to say who I was, he said, 'Jamie. I had a dream you were playin' with your peyote fan. You know you can't do that. You're puttin' yourself and your family in danger.' Next day I got a call from my cousin in Alaska. My dad and my sister were drivin' in a snowstorm and skidded on the ice and crashed. They both died."

From behind the round lenses, tears slid down, one for his dad, one for his sister. They rested on Jamie's cheeks, tiny candle flames dancing in them. I made a mental note not to play with sacred objects.

I told Jamie my mom's dream about my hockey coach and he nodded. "That's all real."

We got around to the Wounded Knee rebellion. He told me the FBI had been hunting down the men who'd fought there. "Two-thirds of the three hundred warriors that fought there are dead, and half of those weren't even drinking." In Oakland, California, agents had cut the brake cables of his car, trying to do away with him, but they killed his wife instead. "I got the drop on the two agents that did it," Jamie told me. "Pointed a pistol at 'em. Tied 'em up and put 'em in a van. Drove 'em out to a lake. Had 'em strip down to their underwear. I said, 'Boys, swim out in the lake. Swim right out there.' And then I did target practice on 'em."

54

"You killed 'em?"

"Yep. I smoked the chanupa a lot by myself after that. We consider it's like a telephone line to the Great Spirit. I smoked it and I talked with Tunkashila and I cried and cried."

Jamie offered to teach me to hunt and make totem poles if I'd stay around and interpret for him. Many times afterward I wished I'd taken him up on his offer, but I had places to go, concepts to investigate, cacti to eat. The villagers said I had *pata de perro*, dog paw—wanderlust. Specifically, at that point I wanted to visit Huichols, famous for their colorful art and their use of peyote. I wanted to systematically derange my senses, or, in Nezahualcoyotl's terms, alter the bandwidth of reality I perceived. So there was no time for totem poles, and the only prey I wanted to hunt was a little green plant.

***

I rode a bus to Guadalajara and stayed with the family from the sun dance. Campeón the Akita was still there, though Novia had run away, and they had a new fluffy little white mutt named Towi, Nahuatl for Boy, who worshipped Campeón like a sports hero. A friend of the family was a veterinarian who worked with Huichols, taking care of their cows and horses, up in the Sierra Madre Occidental, a region of dry hills north of Guadalajara. He wrote me a letter of introduction to a local official. "This young man wishes to know your traditions," it said. "Please treat him as if he were me."

The night before I left, the family stayed up late with me. The moon was full. They remarked that the Aztecs didn't see a man in the moon, but a rabbit. They showed me how to see it, with its two ears silhouetted at the top of the disk. They taught me the Mexican Spanish word for shaman: *curandero*, meaning healer. And they prayed in Spanish to the Great Spirit that I might be successful in my quest, and safe along the way.

I headed off on a series of buses, up into the dry hills for hours and hours on dusty roads. I reached the town that the veterinarian had indicated, and found the municipal meetinghouse. The official I was looking for was out of town, I was told. With a shock, I learned that these people weren't Huichols, but Coras, their less-colorful cousins. My face reddened and I silently swore at the veterinarian for sending me here. A minute later I was able to joke sourly with myself, "That's life. Sometime you get Huichols, sometimes you get Coras." As I knew from my guidebook, the Coras had shamans too. But the Cora tribe had become partly Christianized, and they used peyote only once a year, on Easter, which was months away.

I didn't have any better leads, though, so I decided to stay here and try to find a Cora curandero to visit for a while. Maybe I could try peyote later.

Some people went off and brought back a fourteen-year-old who greeted me in English: "Hey, how are you? Welcome to our town!" Hector had moved back here six months earlier after twelve years with his mom in Los Angeles. He talked about football and rap music, and brought me home to his dad's house. He was nostalgic about Los Angeles, but all things considered, he liked this town better. It was *más tranquilo,* more peaceful. Before we all went to sleep, his dad killed, not one rat, not two, not three, four, five, or even six, but *seven* rats up in the tiled roof with the flat of a machete. Then it was really tranquilo—until I had to relieve myself in the middle of the night, groped my way outdoors in pitch darkness, fell into a ditch, and was suddenly surrounded by all the neighborhood dogs loudly proclaiming that they'd apprehended the world's tallest thief.

Three days later, Hector and I hitchhiked for hours up into the hills until we reached a village called El Nopal where we'd been told a curandero lived. Above the village soared a high, steep hill. When I saw it I wanted to do a vision quest on it. As a kid, I'd often wished I could spend a few days alone in nature. On trips out West with my mom and stepfamily, I'd see hilltops through the car window and want to meditate on them. Later, I learned some North American tribes had initiations for young men that involved praying and fasting alone in places like that. Maybe I could finally do something like that here. The whole area would be quiet and dark at night: it was off the electrical grid. I remembered Nezahualcoyotl's words about mystics: "They don't look for places of power: their destiny takes them there."

Questing after the curandero, Hector and I got the runaround for an hour before being brought back to the first hut compound along the highway where we'd entered the village. Directly across from this compound, an immense boulder guarded the road. We were taken into a hut where a man in his 50s lay on a bed. A pair of handmade crutches leaned against a wall. Tritemio Solís gripped a loop of rope that dangled from a roof beam and pulled himself up into a sitting position to inspect Hector and me. He wore a blue shirt with a collar and a yellow kerchief knotted round his neck. He had medium-length black hair and dark, critical eyes. The eyes of a crow, I thought. In Spanish, I introduced myself and gave the speech I'd planned.

"I'd like to stay here for a while if you'll let me. I'm going around learning about traditional healers. Later, I hope to go south to Ecuador and study with a curandero in the jungle. May I please stay here for a while and learn about your traditions?"

"No."

"Please?"

"No, you can't stay here, it's not OK."

"I've come a long way and I have great respect for your traditions."

"No." Tritemio Solís shook his head firmly.

"All right. Have a good day." I trudged out and plopped down on my backpack. Hector kicked the toe of his sneaker in the dust, wrinkled his nose, bared his teeth, stared at the horizon. He swung his arms behind him, stretched, put his feet together, hopped backwards while rapping in English. A songbird trilled. A goat *baa*ed. A rooster crowed. Insects hummed. Wind swooshed through fragrant pines. No vehicles were going up or down the road that led back to Hector's village. The last one that had passed was the pickup truck that brought us here. I went back to the doorway and said, "I'm sorry. I just want to try one more time. I'm really serious about these things. I'd like to go up on that hill above the village and fast for a few days and pray. I promise I won't make any trouble for you."

At the mention of fasting up on the hill, the curandero's face finally softened, and he nodded.

While Hector waited for a ride back to his village, he and I talked with Tritemio. The rich northerner, I bought bottles of Coke for myself and Hector from our host, and one for the curandero himself, for good measure. His one source of cash, Tritemio told us, was the soft drinks he sold to people passing up or down the road. He explained further that his right femur was fractured. Three days earlier, he'd been the victim of a hit-and-run accident, struck from behind and left unconscious at the side of the road. He didn't know who'd hit him. He added

58

that six months earlier, his wife had died of an unknown ailment in her head.

In this five-room compound, he lived with two of his three sons, a daughter, a daughter-in-law, and a grandson. I could stay in a tiny hut down the hill behind the compound, where his friend Jacinto lived. Jacinto was taking care of him.

A truck was approaching. Hector flagged it down, shook hands with us, and caught a ride back to his town. Tritemio's family drifted back from elsewhere in the village. At dusk, Jacinto appeared—as old as Tritemio, but whiter of skin, grayer of hair, weathered like driftwood, and skinny like the dogs that roamed the village trying to steal tortillas. He and the curandero talked in their language. Tritemio bid me goodnight and I followed Jacinto down to his hut.

The setting sun was flooding the valley with rays. Up above, beyond the road, the cliff of the high hill was reddish-orange against the darkening blue sky. What would I experience up there?

First things first, though. "Where do you guys crap around here?"

"Go over the ridge into the ravine. Take some corn husk with you."

A big pig ambled after me. Orange-pink in the sunset light, he sat atop the ridge, smiling eagerly. *One moment please, sir,* I thought, undoing my belt. *Your dinner will be ready soon.*

By the light of a candle stuck to the white wall by its own wax, Jacinto faced a poster of the Virgin of Guadalupe, and he chanted, gently shaking two wooden wands. Each was tipped with short brown and white feathers. At the end of each wand, where the feather tips were bound with red and green thread, two long brown and white feathers and one rattlesnake rattle dangled down.

When he finished, I asked him what these were.

"They're called *aná*. These feathers," he presented the long ones, "are from the tail of a hawk, and these," the short ones, "from the breast. These *cascabeles* are from rattlesnakes. You can't kill the animals to get these things. The animals have to give them to you."

I nodded, trying to believe him.

He went on, "You look at these anás and you think they're not intelligent, but they're more intelligent than you are. That's how it is." He paused. "By the way, you talk about studying to be a curandero. You better know that if you start, you can't stop without finishing it. If you don't complete the task, you'll be nailing the lid on your own coffin. That's how it is."

He went to sleep on a bed made of ropes strung across a wooden frame and covered with straw mats. I brushed my teeth and, wearing jeans and a jacket, lay on a straw mat on the floor and wrapped myself in a *sarape* I'd bought in Guadalajara—a blanket that has a hole in the middle so you can put your head through it and wear it as a coat—and in two dusty blankets belonging to my host. Jacinto's hut had no door, just an empty metal barrel to block the bottom part of the doorway. The air was frigid. Discomfort and tiredness squabbled over me until tiredness won.

Next morning, Tritemio's 11-year-old son Andrés showed me round the village, then took me out to the edge of it to cut a tree with an axe and bring back the wood for his father's fire. We took turns chopping the dry trunk. I had no aim at all, but kept battering the tree above and below the clean cuts the boy had made. Finally, the tree dropped like a dignified gray ghost into a ravine, from which we dragged it out.

60

In the evening, Andrés's sister-in-law, who was about my age, showed me how to remove dry kernels from an ear of corn with my thumbs. She provided me with a plastic bucket and a big pile of ears of corn. This, I could do. The fire cast a warm light. Everyone was reserved, friendly, curious.

After I'd been there for three days, Jacinto asked me for money in return for staying at his place. "Give me three hundred dollars to start up a little store," he wheedled. "I'm getting old. My wife died years ago. I don't have any children. I have the paperwork in order, I just need to buy the stock. If I can open the store, I can find a wife and I won't have to live out my days alone and in poverty."

"I don't have three hundred dollars," I told him. I had two hundred in pesos and more in traveler's checks. "I can give you one hundred." I brought it out, hefted it.

Thin lips pressed together, eyes on the horizon, Jacinto pocketed the bills without a word.

The next morning, Andrés told me Tritemio had invited me to stay up in his house; I would share a room with Andrés. This was good. The boy had become my guide, my teacher, my student. He was in charge of telling me everything about the village and I was in charge of telling him everything about the world beyond Mexico. Now, I informed him of my transaction with Jacinto. The boy's eyes widened. "That's not his hut! That's *my dad's* hut! And he *does* have kids, they just don't like him!"

Next morning, I ran into Jacinto. Straight-faced, he told me, "One hundred dollars wasn't enough for me to buy stock for a store, so I bought irrigation equipment for my opium plants."

The day after that, Andrés and a neighbor in his 20s and I headed on foot across the dry hills toward a place where we could swim. After a desert hour we came

61

to the edge of a deep canyon dense with vegetation where an ancient river meandered through the earth. Clinging to bamboo stalks, we descended a nearly vertical trail. Under the shelter of a sandstone cliff, just behind the sandy river bank, the neighbor had a garden of tiny opium poppies. He had to return a coiled black hose to someone he'd borrowed it from. That was the purpose, I gathered, of our visit here. The swim was a cover story. Ever the good guest, I carried the hose on my shoulder part of the way down the riverbank. We dropped it off at the base of another steep trail. It dawned on me that everyone around here was growing opium. That might have explained some of Tritemio's initial reluctance to take me in.

Strolling along the narrow riverbank beside the sheer cliff, Andrés and the neighbor spoke disparagingly of bandits.

"What do you mean, 'bandits'?" I asked.

"Bandits," Andrés explained, "steal other people's opium."

Overheated and dusty, the three of us did finally swim, in a vast, shaded bowl of sandstone sculpted by eons of river. It was fantastic. To bathe in the village, you had to squat next to a rivulet and pour water over yourself with a cup.

***

In my journal, Andrés sketched the village. At the bottom, in the area where no one lived because it was too far down the slope, he drew a series of five opium poppies at different stages of development. He sketched his dad's compound with three figures: himself, his three-year-old nephew, and me. He sketched animals that lived in the vicinity, appending their names in Cora:

the scorpion, *tashka;*

the rattlesnake, *cucu;*
the lizard, *yana;*
the centipede, *nazbeme.*

He sketched a self-portrait, which was strikingly accurate apart from the fact that he portrayed himself wearing two sandals, when in fact he had only one.

He sketched the boulder next to the road outside his house, adding a giant scorpion perched atop it. "That boulder is *el Patrón de Alacranes,*" he said—the boss of scorpions. "We give it cornmeal once a year and ask it to protect us from getting stung."

Another time he pointed out little wooden shelves behind houses, and explained that people put cornmeal out on those, too, to feed their deceased relatives' spirits when they came around. I imagined importing the idea to the United States and marketing it next to birdfeeders as a deadfeeder. Or simply building one for my mom so she could leave steak and boiled potatoes for her brother Pat.

Sitting with Tritemio one morning, I brought up my idea to fast from food and water on the hill above the village. He said that it would be fine, and that the hill was a site where Huichols stopped and offered prayers while they were on pilgrimage. When I was ready to go, he lent me a cloth pouch of locally-grown tobacco and a ceramic pipe with a bamboo stem.

I hiked up the steep hill on its network of goat paths. At the top, I found a cairn Huichols had built with weathered offerings inside: a yarn painting in a gourd, and a pair of god's eyes, little wooden plus signs wrapped with yarn to make multicolored concentric squares.

On a bed of one blanket and my sarape, with a sweater for a pillow, I lay and stared up at the clouds. My dream of fasting on a hilltop was coming true.

Nezahualcoyotl, I spoke, entrusting my voice to the wind, *thank you for your counsel. Fasting Coyote, I'm fasting with the coyotes too, now.*

Coyotes fast a lot, I realized as an afterthought. *It's clearly no problem for them to go without food for a few days. It keeps them sharp and sensitive. Great Spirit, grant me some of their sharpness and sensitivity.*

Time flowed like air. I cloud-drifted above ordinary life, high among solemn, silent companions: hunger, thirst, plants, stones, dreams, sky. I saw faces in clouds and Hebrew letters in tree branches. I wrote love letters to Lily and made long lists of foods we could eat together. Flavors from my childhood flooded back—the cream-filled chocolate eggs from the Easter baskets my mom had assembled for me; the bowls of cottage cheese, sour cream, and fruit cocktail my dad used to give me as a snack when I visited his apartment every other weekend and every other Thursday afternoon, as ordered by the court.

I promised myself that when I got home I'd open a big can of peaches in heavy syrup and, as quickly as possible, eat them all and drink the syrup. Again and again, I imagined doing this.

Three days and three nights passed, and it was time to go back down into the village.

A week later, I went up on the hill a second time and fasted for four days and nights. It was even harder, but I felt I was making progress.

On the last evening, I filled Tritemio's pipe with tobacco and faced the sunset. As I smoked, I prayed as Jamie Bear had taught me: "Great Spirit, please grant me a vision and the power to heal." I imagined that vision flooding into me, washing the shadows out of my heart, filling me with a gentle, brilliant light that I could then channel to others. Afterwards, I stood up too fast and got a head rush.

***

I sway, dizzy, staring around. I've passed through the gate. I'm in the spirit world. It's been expecting me, and preparing for me as I've been preparing for it. The air is thick as water, and my surroundings quietly, consciously, watch me.

***

Gradually, the effect wore off. I prayed again and bedded down for the night, tasting the bitter, comforting residue of *Nicotiana rustica* in my mouth.

Next morning, lightheaded and encouraged, I picked my way back down the goat paths. The sky was electric blue and the dry hills soaked with buttery light.

Welcome, I echoed Nezahualcoyotl. *I want more.*

***

Back at Tritemio's, I assembled makeshift beds of empty plastic Coca Cola crates for Andrés and me. They were marginally softer than the cement floor.

Some dawns I woke to the sound of Tritemio gently singing in his language in the open area between the rooms.

I did simple chores. I was good enough at *granando*, prying the dried corn off the cob with my thumbs so it could be soaked, ground, and made into tortillas. But I was the most inept woodcutter the village had ever seen. All the wood was twisted and hard. Everyone was an expert at placing an axe blade in exactly the right place to split it. I gave myself blisters battering the wood.

65

I was better at singing Beatles songs—a legacy of a car trip across Canada with my dad when I was ten. I taught Andrés to accompany me on the chorus of "Lucy in the Sky with Diamonds," which he did tunefully and with gusto, though he pronounced it "Lucy in the sky with diamonish."

"Diamonds," I said.

"Diamonish," Andrés repeated, his brow furrowed.

"Listen. Diamon-*ds*," I enunciated, slowing it down.

"Diamon-*ish!*" Laughter burst out between the boy's big white teeth.

I couldn't pronounce his language well either. It had a consonant between l, r, and zh that I couldn't hit no matter how many times I tried.

My reaction to the Coras' opium growing was negative, but I remembered that these were poor people on poor land with poor opportunities, independently of whatever that meant for their souls. According to my guidebook, the tribe had retreated from the Spanish up into these inhospitable hills at the time of the conquest of Mexico in the early 1500s. Led by a man they called the Nayar, the Sun King, the Coras formed a strong union out of a group of squabbling tribes and headquartered themselves up in a town later named La Mesa del Nayar— the flat-topped mountain of the Sun King—in order to defend themselves against their common enemy. They were able to stay independent for two centuries until the third Spanish army that attacked them finally broke their resistance in 1722. The Spaniards captured and burned the Nayar's mummified body, but not his skull, which was smuggled deep into a cave. Jesuit priests moved in and Christianized the Coras before being expelled from the Spanish colonies in 1768. The tribe had always survived, but the soil in the hills was dry, and they'd never experienced prosperity.

I said to Tritemio, "You shouldn't grow opium. It's really bad. You should grow marijuana instead. Do you know what that is?"

"Yes, but it's much worse than opium. It makes people go insane."

I thought, "Look at me, I smoke it and I'm not insane," but I couldn't imagine a positive outcome to a conversation like that, so I just said, "OK."

Early one morning Tritemio's older son and a friend rode away early on horseback. They cantered back in mid-afternoon, elated, their faces bee-stung and swollen. They carried big white plastic buckets full of dripping honeycombs.

As we sat squeezing out the wax and feasting on the honey, it occurred to me that these poor people were no less happy than the wealthier people I knew in the States. In fact, they seemed happier. They had three major problems I could identify. One was the lack of variety in their diet. Most days they ate nothing but corn tortillas and salt, and drank nothing but water and instant coffee. They ate only twice a day, once at dawn and once after dusk—though, admittedly, their fresh, homemade tortillas were the best I had ever had. The second problem was that without money, they couldn't travel much. The third problem was the lack of medical care. Maybe Tritemio's wife would have survived if she'd been able to go to a hospital. My mom's question resonated: If shamanism can't save lives, what good is it?

Tritemio was fond of sitting in a kind of rough Adirondack chair under the roof of his compound and gazing off into the distance. A low, broad valley extended there, and after a bright, hot day, the sunset reddened the hills.

I saw him sad only one day. That day he was heartbroken from morning to night. I didn't ask about it and he didn't volunteer anything. His sister came to visit in the evening and sat with him quietly in the kitchen for a long time.

A different day, while I was granando, flipping the corn kernels into a plastic bucket between my feet, Tritemio was standing nearby, leaning on his crutches, looking into the distance. I asked him how people became healers in his tribe. His crow eyes brightened and he hobbled near and spoke animatedly. "First you have to go to the church in La Mesa del Nayar in the middle of the night and ask Jesus for permission to be a healer. Then you have to go to the mouth of the earth, a cave we call Tuacamota. Fast there, five days and nights. You can't sleep, just pray, and sit up all night. On the last night, four animals will come to you, one at a time. Huge, terrifying animals."

Smiling broadly, he started to tip over. I leapt up and grabbed his shoulders and steadied him. He went on, still smiling. "Huge, terrifying animals. A bear, a bull, a puma, and a snake. You have to sit there. Each gives you a spiritual gift. For example, the snake sticks out its tongue and you have to touch it with your own tongue. This gives you the ability to understand the languages of animals and birds. If you get scared and run away from the huge, magical animals, you go insane for a few days. Maybe your family has to go and find you. And you lose your chance to be a healer." He gazed into the distance again. "Me, I just sat there and accepted the gifts, despite my fear. Now, there's another kind of initiation that happens when you travel to the desert with the Huichols, to the place they call Wirikuta or Wirimota. I did that too. You go to the desert and look for peyote. You pray and ask it to appear. If it wants you to find it, you do. When you eat peyote, there's no teacher, it's the *Patrones* that teach you, out there by yourself in the desert." I remembered Andrés using the

68

word *Patrón* for that scorpion spirit boulder. It seemed to refer to a spiritual being higher up a chain of authority—like Jacinto's anás.

The Cora initiation would require too much involvement, and though I hadn't found any Huichols, I wanted to get to that peyote desert and meet the Patrones. I sent the wish out like a prayer: *Patrones, if you exist, please show yourselves to me. I seek you in as proper a way as I can.* I'd been in El Nopal for a month, and I got ready to leave.

My last night at Tritemio's place, a mom brought her son over for a healing. He was about eight. He had white bumps on his tongue, Tritemio told me, and found it very painful to eat. The mom went in the kitchen to visit with the shaman's daughter and daughter-in-law. Tritemio fed a couple more pieces of resinous pine heartwood to the fire and had the boy stand on a chair.

Tritemio packed a pipe full of tobacco, ignited it, murmured a prayer, and blew smoke to each of the four directions. Then he had the boy stick out his tongue. The curandero leaned in close and sucked on the tongue with a whoosh of air. He backed up and spat on the ground, took a puff off the pipe, and moved in and sucked again, repeating this treatment for ten or fifteen minutes, completely focused on getting the sickness out of that tongue.

It looked sort of like pedophilia but there was zero sexuality in it. Instead, it seemed a behavior based on an older concept of bodies and personal space than the one in my society.

I never found out if the treatment had any effect. In the morning I said goodbye to everyone and hitchhiked away through the dry hills.

***

My destination was Real de Catorce, a town with two claims to fame. One, it was a silver mining boom town in the 1880s, with 20,000 inhabitants, but then the silver ran out and the population dropped to 800, so for the most part it's a ghost town. The other thing is that it's perched at the edge of the mountains next to the desert flatland of Wirikuta. I hoped to meet the cacti and the Patrones. Then I would fly out of Mexico to Ecuador, where I hoped to meet a shaman I could study with.

The Coca-Cola truck I rode out of El Nopal dropped me in a town called Jesús María. The residents were Coras and mestizos. A mestizo cowboy my age invited me to stay at his place. He loved Country and Western music and wanted to know all about the United States. I told him all I could, explaining Democrats and Republicans, the Revolutionary War, the Declaration of Independence, the Constitution, manifest destiny, the Civil War....

Next day, I washed my clothes by hand in the river, then spread them out on some rocks to dry in the sun and sat down to write in my journal. A big pig drifted by like a meaty cloud on trotters, foraging, and, I thought, smiling at me. When the pig was gone, I looked up and found that my new pink bar of laundry soap had vanished. I checked around the stones and couldn't find it. It had apparently walked away with the pig. I read the empty wrapper. The main ingredient was lard.

On the road, an army officer in his late twenties approached me. "I'm in charge of drug enforcement around here," he said. "Do you know where the Indians are growing opium?"

"No," I lied.

"Do you smoke marijuana?" he asked.

"Yes, but not around here, only in my own country," I said, thinking it wouldn't kill me to be honest. "Do you?"

"Yes, all of us soldiers do."

This confused me. "So, you raid a field, and confiscate the marijuana on it, and then you smoke it?"

"No, no!" He was shocked. "First we *dry* it! *Then* we smoke it."

He invited me to the base for a game of volleyball, and later dared me to cut the head off a black rooster he and his men were going to have for dinner. They hung the bird from a nail on a wooden post by a piece of twine around its feet. One soldier held the head still for me. The officer passed me a kitchen knife. I took a deep breath and sawed through the feathery neck as fast as I could. Blood Jackson Pollacked the dusty ground. Powerful wings flapped madly, subsided. "Well done," said the officer, and started ripping fistfuls of black feathers from the corpse.

***

In front of the local branch of the National Indigenous Institute, I was drinking Dos Equis with the thirtysomething director and his eighteenish girlfriend. "This week I'm organizing transportation for some Huichols," the man said. "They're going on a pilgrimage to the desert where the peyote grows. Wirikuta, they call it. We've got two trucks, and funding for gasoline. We're gonna bring them over there. Five hundred kilometers."

"No way!" I said. "I've read about their peyote pilgrimages. And I want to go to Wirikuta. Could I go too?"

"Sure thing! No problem! We leave in three days!"

71

Later, we all went to a party, and a guy whose face I couldn't see in the dark asked me if I wanted to work for him transporting opium along the highway. *No, gracias.*

In the morning I told my host about the Huichol pilgrimage. He was happy for me and told me I was welcome to stay until it set off.

But over the next week, the Huichols who trickled in from their village postponed the departure date again and again, using various cryptic excuses. I was frustrated. Adrift. Baffled. To cheer myself up I ate *tacos de chorizo* every day, spending more money than I'd budgeted. I was haunted by Jacinto's claim that I'd die if I didn't finish my shamanic education. I wrote anxious letters to Lily. Finally I gave up on the Huichols and hitchhiked out of Jesús María on my own.

8. Station Fourteen

A few days later, I was dropped off on a sunny street in Real de Catorce. A brown-dreadlocked gringa with a long, slender neck and a monobrow was walking in the shadow of a ruined stone wall atop which prickly pear cacti grew. I said, "'Scuse me, do you know where there's a hotel around here?"

"Next street over," she said. She smelled of patchouli and sweat. I was attracted. "Come on," she said. "I'm going there. It's where my husband and I are staying. Well, he's not actually my husband. We just say we're married so we don't get any problems with the people around here. They can be pretty conservative."

"I understand. That's a good idea. Why'd you come to Mexico?"

"Lots of reasons," she said. "To work on my art. I was a studio art major at UC Santa Cruz. To learn to see the night sky in three dimensions, and paint that. To work on my tan. To read the legends in cricket songs. To stroke the skin of the clouds."

"I take it you're a poet and a peyote eater, too?"

"I'm sort of a poet, and I eat peyote pretty much when I can, unless I'm having a rosebleed. Last reason to be here is to get away from American advertising. Seems like every time there's a TV on, some dude is screamin' at you to buy shit. 'It's the Ford summer sales event of a lifetime! Act now, while supplies last!' I'm like, 'No, fuck you! Kiss my ass! Down with capitalism! Smash the patriarchy!' Know what I mean? Haven't spoken English in a while. It tends to come out in a rush."

"I know just what you mean," I said, "and I totally agree. My name's Nathan, by the way."

"Lisa."

We shook hands and walked to the hotel. Lisa banged on a door. The owner wasn't in. I surveyed the place, a collection of run-down buildings and a pig pen around a courtyard. The pen was pigged by a peaceful, gargantuan, white-haired beast lying in a sunbeam in the mud with an almost-human smile on his lips. "They're fattening him up to kill him for Easter," Lisa murmured. "A lot of people are going to eat him."

"What a life he has," I said. "All he has to do is eat and lie in the sun. And then, he'll die."

"I've sketched him a lot," Lisa said. "I want to do an oil painting of him."

"Good idea."

"I think he knows what the deal is," she went on, "and he's OK with it."

"That reminds me," I said, "of those young Aztec guys who got treated as living gods for a year and then sacrificed."

Lisa said, "We had something like that already. One morning a couple weeks ago we woke up to these terrifying screams. I thought someone was being murdered! Turned out they were castrating the pig. There was blood all over the walls and paving stones in the courtyard."

The pig stood up like a snowy mountain, stretched and trembled, stood still a while, then sat down in the cool mud in the shade and plopped over on his side.

"Let me see your sketches?"

We sat in the sun with our backs against a stone wall as I leafed through her sketchpad. Along with the inevitable trippy patterns, stars, eyeballs, wave forms, skulls, rainbows, and the like, there were drawings that sought a likeness of things—the flesh-mountain of the pig, the spiky ovals that made up nopal cacti, the angular ruins of the curious old town. But the images seemed, in a word, *sketchy*. Undefined. Indefinite. Like she was seeking to pin them down on the page, but they were moving too fast. Were they trembling? Or straining to fly back to the objects from which they had been drawn? *Hmm*, I said, nodding and half-smiling. I wondered what my dad the art teacher would say about the sketches. They showed some talent, I thought, but fell disappointingly short of greatness. Several showed a young man's dark face with black hair pulled back in a ponytail. The cheeks were fat, the nose was broad, the nostrils flaring, the eyes heavy-lidded; a single vertical crease marked the space between the eyebrows, slightly to the left of the center. "Mario," Lisa explained.

As if on cue, Mario himself walked out of their room, barefoot, with the bearing of a martial artist who may be a musician, or vise-versa. In decent Spanish, Lisa introduced us. Some tension in his voice showed he was jealous about my chatting with his lady. But after some wheedling on my part—which mentioned my quest for indigenous wisdom, and contained the word *hermano* and the observation that he and I were both hippies—he disappeared and reappeared with a peyote button for me to eat.

I held the spineless cactus in the palm of my hand, examining its jade-like roundness in the sunlight, silently sending it greetings and blessings. As I eased it into my mouth and began to crush it between my teeth, I noticed Mario beginning to roll a joint.

The cactus's flesh was intensely bitter, but fresh, lively. I couldn't chew without grimacing. *Pe-YO-te*, I thought as I chewed. *Onomatopoeia. The name is the sound of a soft, living emerald. Onomatopeyote.*

75

The plant and I thought about each other. Silent conversation flowed between us. His mind was much older than mine. No wonder the indigenous people called him Grandfather.

Mario licked the rolling paper, sealed the joint, placed it on a stone to dry in the sun, murmured a few words in Spanish to Lisa, who produced a pink plastic lighter and stretched her toes in the sunlight before grinning at me.

Sucking the last of the cactus from my teeth, I sat on the warm stones of the sun-soaked courtyard in the company of these two new friends, as the joint with its delicious, pungent smoke went around.

***

The ganja takes effect. Mario's heavy-lidded eyes half-smile. Lisa squeezes his hand, golden skin on reddish brown. The moment becomes timeless. I'm Leon Trotsky meeting Frida Kahlo and Diego Rivera, again and again, in body after body, down through time. And the joint is a wizard squid with tentacles of smoke, shrinking, bit by bit, as it employs our fingers and a dash of Kabbala to fly through the air and bind our stories together for these moments.

"Sssssssssssso," says Mario, exhaling a stream of smoke in a whisper that's also a sigh, as he passes the spliff to Lisa. He meets my swamp-green eyes with his earth-brown ones. "You are seeking the wisdom of the indigenous people. The thing to know is this." Aztec-warrior-like, he furrows his brow, deepening the crease on the left, summoning words. I look away. My eyes meet a tendril of white cloud made gold by the sun in the blue sky. Mario's voice says, "It's simply that the indigenous people notice what others don't."

"Ah." I nod. That seems incredibly profound. I flash back to the face of one of the Huichols last week in Jesus María. With a shock, I finally read its expression, and its implication: he and his friends were waiting for me to leave! They didn't want a stranger along on their pilgrimage!

Ah! I've been a fool again, I reflect with a rueful smile. *Like the Fool on the Tarot card.*

Under a bright sun, a young wanderer strolls close to the edge of a cliff, nearly falling off. But his innocence protects him. He still has to learn about himself and the world through many adventures.

I pick up the sketchbook again. Now the pages are huge microscope slides of thin slices of time. The lines that seek the outline of the body of the pig refuse false realism: instead, Lisa has given them freedom to express the potential of the shape, like electrons that may be anywhere around a nucleus. Brilliant, spectacular, nearly everywhere at once.

I feed my eyes, then close them and the sketchbook and lean back against the warm stone wall.

The sun is full of ecstatic people working hard to create heat and light. They smile and wave at me, glad I can see them through the orange of my eyelids. I raise my palms to their innumerable, Nezahualcoyotlian energies, and smile back, thinking, *Thank you. Give me more.*

***

Next morning, I met another gringo peyote-seeker, John from Las Vegas, a big-bellied hippie businessman in whose beard and ponytail reddish-brown was losing the war to gray. We decided to join forces, and planned our strategy.

Real de Catorce is perched on a hill above a desert which the Coras and Huichols call Wirikuta, where peyote plants grow, dusty jade mandalas under low, scrubby creosote bushes.

The following day, we would take one of the ancient deathtrap taxis my guidebook described down the steep road from Real de Catorce to the village of Estación Catorce. There was a railway station, and lodgings. Mario gave me the address of a family-run hotel. From there, we'd enter the desert to hunt peyote.

That evening I was dining alone in a chilly, drafty restaurant when two Italian travelers blew in. In Spanish, I invited them to my table, the most sheltered from the wind. The younger one, like a white Bob Marley, brown dreadlocks bracketing his freckled, goateed face, said, "We won't bother you?"

"We'll see if you do or not," I said with a smile. I was pretty sure they wouldn't.

I was wrong. The older Italian, Mauricio, balding and thinly mustached, went off on Jews. "They deserved what happened to them in World War Two," he said. "They're dishonest. That makes them ashamed of themselves, and afraid. Look around Latin America. They never travel alone, always in big crowds."

"Look at me," I said. "Do you see a big crowd of Jews around me? What you're looking at is a Jew traveling alone. And there's good and bad in every group. It's no reason to commit genocide. Tell me, are all Italians honest?"

Mauricio hesitated, then muttered something I didn't understand. His younger companion, Franco, stepped in and rescued the evening by regaling us with tales of Titicaca, a huge, high-altitude lake in Bolivia, where people lived on floating islands made of reeds.

After dinner, I invited the Italians to join John's and my move to Estación Catorce. They said sure.

In the morning, I said goodbye to Lisa and Mario, and the three other travelers and I headed down the maddeningly steep road in a rattling black taxi piloted by a local with a jaw like Frankenstein's monster. We gripped the door handles, ready to spring out if the brakes failed—which, of course, they didn't. Eventually the taxi reached level ground, like a plane landing. And we checked into the tiny hotel that Mario had recommended.

It was run by a Señora Sabas, a merry, blue-eyed old lady out of a fairy tale. Wierdly for us, she was ready to lodge us all in one room with two double beds because she thought that like her Mexican clientele, we would want to save money that way. We explained it wasn't our custom to sleep two in a bed. The Italians shacked up together, and John and I moved into a two-bed room. Peyote seekers had covered the walls with graffiti. *"Muerto estarás mejor,"* noted one scrawl, next to a sketch of an object that was part skull, part peyote cactus—"You'll be better off dead." I felt cheered by the thought: something to look forward to. John, stretching out on his warm bed near a sunny window, remarked, "This is better than the Hilton." Equally pleased, I took out a felt-tip pen and wrote on the wall, "Better than the Hilton."

Also on the wall was an electricity meter labeled "Watthorímetro Thermofascio." It dovetailed with something I'd been thinking about: how strange it must have seemed to the Coras that someone from the distant, incomprehensible United States wanted to learn to be a shaman. It was as if a young billionaire from outer space, eight feet tall, completely lacking in muscle tone, incapable of doing tasks as simple as opening a twist tie, and as pale as a sheet of paper, appeared in Brooklyn and went to the

Lubovicher Hasidim claiming he needed to become a rabbi.

I imagined writing a science fiction story about this. The visitor's name would sound as weird to the Hasidim as mine did to the Coras: Watthorímetro Thermofascio. The Hasidim would be surprised and skeptical that Watt wanted to become a rabbi, but seeing that he was serious about it, and willing to share a pinch of his fortune, they would take in the young space traveler and study Talmud with him and maybe even help him convert to Judaism.

Exploring outside our room, John and I met a skinny Mexican hippie in his late 20s scrubbing a pair of jeans in an outdoor sink. Alberto looked about 65% Spanish and 35% indigenous; had a thin black mustache; wore a straw hat with a silver chain for a band. Said he had a general idea where the peyote grew because he'd been here the previous year. And sure, we could go with him.

As the conversation developed, he and I realized our paths had nearly crossed before. When Nezahualcoyotl held the sun dance in Ajijic, Alberto had been in a cave in the same hill, eating peyote and meditating.

***

John, Franco, Alberto, and I walked into the desert while Mauricio the anti-Semite stayed behind to take pictures of the 19th century cemetery. I silently paraphrased Jesus: *Let the dead photograph the dead.*

A car was coming from the village. Alberto flagged it down. There was no room inside, but Alberto got them to agree to let us stand on the back bumper and grip the smooth roof. When the car started up again, John immediately fell off. The driver stopped. John got back up and gripped my arm to help stay on, actually whimpering with fear. He nearly yanked me off as the car gathered speed. But I was feeling fine—I was going to seek the peyote—and my palms had a firm grip on the roof. I figured the road must be smooth or they wouldn't have let us ride back here.

Ten minutes later, Alberto tapped the roof twice. The driver stopped and let us off. We headed out among the creosote bushes, peering around. After a long time, John found a single peyote cactus. He knelt and cut it as Alberto stipulated: just the top, so the root would regenerate. He gave it to me. I silently greeted Grandfather Peyote, ate the bitter emerald jelly stone, and gauged the blue of the sky to see if it would intensify later. We kept on walking and searching, searching and walking. I'd been fasting that day: nothing but a glass of water in the morning. The peyote took away my hunger and thirst; when I asked my body about this, I got the answer that everything was being taken care of. But where were the rest of the cacti we were looking for?

"Franco," I said. "The Huichols confess their sins when they go to hunt the peyote. They say it purifies them and makes them more acceptable to the good spirits. Could I confess a sin to you?"

"Sure, if you want. I have a sin too."

"In my first year at university, I had a relationship with a girl. She studied the flute. One night, something happened between us. And she left the university the next day. I never saw her again. She left me a note that said, 'What you did last night was like rape.' Those were her exact words. Not rape, but *like* rape. I phoned her at her parents' house two years later and we said we forgave each other. It seemed about half true. But that incident was so crazy and bad, it still fucks up my life to this day. I'm sure it does hers, too. Sometimes I wish I was in prison so I

81

could pay for the crime and get it over with. As it is, I feel like I'm gonna carry it around forever."

"Just keep punishing yourself," Franco said, almost cheerfully. "You'll feel better eventually. For me, my worst sin was injecting drugs. I was so, so, so stupid. Nearly killed myself. It made me see how connected people are. Because when I fell, I started to pull other people down with me. Like I was falling into a hole in the earth, and drawing them into it—my family, friends, girlfriend. Luckily, they fought it. It took a lot of work by the people around me to pull me out and get me back on my feet. My girlfriend was gone when I recovered, but that was all right."

***

After two and a half hours of searching, we stopped to rest under a solitary tree. Between the four of us, we'd found nothing but the one button John had given me. We'd have to think about heading back into town before long, so as not to be out in the desert when night fell.

As the others knew, this was my only chance to eat peyote. I was taking the train out of Estación Catorce the following morning and making my way back to Guadalajara and then Mexico City to catch a flight to Ecuador where the ayahuasca grew.

Under the lonesome tree, we shared an orange that Franco had brought along. Then Alberto rolled a joint, lit it, and released the kabbalistic squid to fly smoky circles in our midst—once, twice, thrice....

John takes a big hit and passes to me. I hit and pass to Alberto. John's cheeks and eyes bulge comically as he holds in his too-big hit. Then smoke jets out his nose and he coughs. When he catches his breath again, he laughs with an Arizonian *Haw!* Franco takes a drag, slow and reggae-cool.

Soon, the joint's too small to smoke anymore. Franco stubs it out. It looks like a dead moth.

"What are the words in your languages for when it gets too small to smoke?" I ask. "In English, we call it a roach, short for cockroach—a *cucaracha.*"

"We say *bachita,*" says Alberto.

"In Italian, *cicca,*" says Franco.

I say, "Ah, but what does the cicca call itself?"

Franco inquires of the bit of paper-wrapped plant, *"Oye, perdón, pero ¿cómo te llamas?"* But there's no answer but the whisper of the breeze in the tree. The creature has already spoken, exhaling its molecules into our bepotted minds.

Franco hands it to Alberto and says in Spanish, "I wonder how many words there've been for this in all the languages."

Alberto stows it in his shirt pocket and says, "Sometimes a word is spoken only once and then forgotten."

Franco says, "That's how memory is."

There's a long pause, the air trembling with forgotten names and others that don't yet exist.

Franco exclaims, "I almost forgot, we're looking for peyote!" He and Alberto and I burst out laughing. John smiles indulgently, not understanding the Spanish.

Ashamed of my weirdness even now, I screw up my courage and say, "Look, I've been studying the indigenous people's traditions, and they say the peyote lets you find it if it wants you to. And they try to pray and get in tune with their environment, and they talk to the peyote with their hearts and tell it why they want to find it. So what would you-all think if we prayed a little?"

They agree. Franco produces a Bolivian flute from his knapsack and blows whispery notes. I summon my memories of Nezahualcoyotl, Jamie, and Tritemio, then speak in the direction of the sky: "Tunkashila! Dios! Elohim! Mother Earth! Great Spirit! This is your grandson Nathan. I'm here with your other grandsons John, Alberto, Franco. We've come here from far away. We've come with pure intentions, wanting to find some peyote to help us get a vision of how we can proceed with our lives. Great Spirit, we're hurting in so many ways. Sometimes we get frustrated, not knowing what to do, how to behave, how to live correctly. We've done bad things. We don't want to do bad things anymore. We're carrying around so much pain. We want to let it go. We want to walk your path. We want to be better men. Please, if it's your will, share with us some of your sacred medicine and help us learn to heal our hearts and live in the best possible way, not only for ourselves, but for you and for all your creations. Aho."

We remain still for a few minutes while the heat gilds us and the sunlight falls in trembling patches between the leaves of the tree. We feel the earth, we smell its dust. We feel the breeze, and our memories, touching our skin and hair. We think invisible multicolored thoughts, birds of a desert paradise.

We stand and stretch. Barely ten seconds later, Alberto exclaims, *"Ah, ¡aquí está!"* He bends to cut three jade-green buttons growing together in a clump. We begin to find them all around, now here, now there, as many as we wish, and we kneel to harvest them, and, too, to eat them.

Franco finds the largest specimen. It looks so much like the face of a smiling clown that I take a photo of it, convinced that this will prove, once and for all, the validity of shamanism and the existence of the supernatural.

(Twenty-one years later, I will reencounter the photo and conclude it doesn't look anything like a clown; more like a smiling lizard—but not even very much like a smiling lizard; most like a cactus.)

We're walking on the road in the direction of Estación Catorce when John says, "Ya know, it sounds crazy, but it almost seems like praying helped us find the peyote."

Through a bitter mouthful of cactus, I mutter, "Yeah! What do you think?"

We walk on a few paces.

John scratches his chin, tugs his red, brown, and white beard, and says, "I wish we had a ride back into town."

"Why don't you pray for one?"

"Hmm," he says.

Soon a pickup stops for us and we climb in the back and the driver speeds toward Estación Catorce.

I've read that peyote can amplify one's sense of balance, and I find it true. As we zoom down the road, I stand calmly, not holding on to anything, chatting with the others, keeping an eye on the smooth road ahead. Then the people in the cab wave frantically at me to sit down. Well, OK.

Back in town, we find Mauricio having a very civilized chicken dinner at a tiny square metal table outside a tiny restaurant. For some, the anti-Semite will be the true hero of these writings, but, unfortunately, this is the last we see of him, though I will recall him on a train the next morning. John and I stock up on corn tortillas and cheese at a store and return to the hotel, while Alberto and Franco stay in town to look for *mota*, weed.

John eats, showers, and goes to bed early in a room that's far better than the Hilton. After the long hike, he

85

falls asleep almost before his head hits the pillow, which transforms for him into a giant pale-green peyote button.

Alberto and Franco get back to the hotel and the three of us go to Alberto's room. They unwrap a piece of newspaper with half an ounce of weed in it and start to roll joints. At the fireplace in the corner of the room, wielding newspaper, wood, and matches, I light a fire, then melt cheese over tortillas and feed the three of us.

Eating peyote on the slow and steady, one button per hour, I pass up the pungent flying squids of mota that circulate, diffusing their quirky molecular wisdom to us thick-headed primates.

Well, I pass up the squids about half the time. I'm focused on the peyote. But he and the cannabis seem friendly to one another.

Our hearing sweetened by the herb, we want music. Alberto produces a guitar and photocopies of Beatles lyrics; between conversations in Spanish, we sing.

After the last chord of *Lady Madonna* fades, Franco says, "I feel sort of nauseated from the peyote. I wonder if I should make myself throw up."

Alberto says, "Sometimes it's best to just let it settle."

I say, "No, it's always better to vomit. Even if you feel just a little nauseated when you're in the middle of the city, like on the steps outside a bank." I mime puking. "'Terribly sorry, madam, I simply must purify myself, you know!'" My companions cackle with laughter.

Whether a short time or a long time passes, no-one knows, but we're all leaning forward with our elbows on our knees, Franco and I listening to Alberto philosophize. "We have," the Mexican says, "an indigenous concept embodied in the word *inlakesh*. That means 'I'm another you.' Inlakesh implies that anything you do to me, you do to yourself, and anything I do to you, I do to myself. It's a

way we have of remembering to treat each other well."
Franco and I nod, digesting the information. Neither of us
other hims has any questions.

Then Franco—or the boundless, eternal soul
energy that temporarily resides in the body by that name—
must be feeling better, because he stands up and stretches
and shakes his dreadlocks and inquires petulantly of the
rest of the universe, "I wonder if there's any place in town
that would be open to sell me a beer right now."

"Of course there isn't," says Alberto, his eyes wide.
"The village is much too small. We're probably the only
people awake at midnight anyway." The Mexican, who's
ordinarily very laid-back, lays his guitar on his bed and says
to me, "Look at this guy! Half an ounce of dope and
dozens of peyote buttons on the table, and all this fucking
Italian can think about is beer?" *Nos cagamos de risa*, as the
Latinos say—we all shit ourselves laughing. Wiping tears
off his cheeks, Franco wistfully rolls another joint.

I head outside to look at the stars. Señora Sabas is
standing at the gate. "What are you doing?" she quizzes,
her pale blue eyes sapphires in the streetlight.

"When one eats peyote, one often has the urge to
go look at the stars," I say.

"I never took peyote," she says.

"Cada quien a su gusto," I say. To each his own.

She says, "You're probably wondering why I have
blue eyes. Most people do. They don't say it, but I see the
question in *their* eyes. Were you wondering?"

"Yes, of course."

"I inherited them from my German grandfather.
He was a mining engineer from Hessia who came here for
the silver boom."

"German eyes, looking out on a Mexican
landscape."

87

"Yes. And what are you doing in this Mexican landscape, young man?"

"Trying to learn to be a curandero. A shaman. Someone who eats these plants to see visions that can be helpful."

"Very nice," she says. "Well, don't let me keep you from your star gazing."

"Good night, ma'am!"

"Good night, sir!"

I stride through the village, sneakers crunching gravel, remembering another night years ago when I trudged a spiral in the snow of a frozen lake.

I halt, rest my hands on my hips, flex my back, feeling like a cartoon character. Run a hand through my dusty hair, look up at the stars, wonder about my life. Where am I going to live? How will I earn a living? What's going to happen when I get to Ecuador? How am I ever going to ever heal myself? Will I always hurt? Will I marry Lily? Someone else? No one? Will I have kids? What kind of father could I be? How can I be responsible for others when I can barely take care of myself?

I peer up at the stars, but they tell me nothing I can understand. They just sway there, drifting: bioluminescent fish in a black ocean.

Great Spirit, grant me a vision and the power to heal. Illuminate the path I'm here to take. Grant me a vision so bright it'll blow the shadows out of my soul.

I don't want to live in darkness anymore. Either let me move forward, or kill me once and for all.

I circle back and enter Alberto's room. A fragrant stank of weedage welcomes me. Franco, leaning back, eyes closed, smiling, listens to our host strumming and singing,

"*Yo*

soy

el

y eres

el

y eres

yo

y todos

somos

juntos

...”

The herb has narrowed the men's eyes and widened
their smiles. I eat one last peyote button, the head of a
sage reptile. That makes one per hour for fourteen hours.
That's the right number, I think. *Fourteen hours, fourteen buttons,
and fourteen's in the names of these towns.* Real de Catorce,
Royal of Fourteen; Estación Catorce, Station Fourteen.
My guidebook says no one's sure how those names
happened. In any case, the official number of this place.

As the last chord of *Yo soy el morso* fades in the calm
air, a motor is heard. It stops. Doors open and slam.
Voices! Boisterous voices!

"They sound like they might be speaking Italian!"
says Franco, leaping up. "Maybe we can have a football
game, Italians against Mexicans!"

Señora Sabas's voice calls, "Alberto, you have
visitors. I'm going to make up rooms for them. But they
say they know you."

Moments later, six Mexican hippies flood into
Alberto's room. They share organic baked goods and
speak of mysticism and peyote. "On the way from
Guadalajara," the leader says, "we explored this *fucked-up*
ruined pre-Colombian town! It's called La Quemada 'cause
it was destroyed by fire. Totally crazy!"

The room is suddenly too loud and too full. Can't
have people bringing down my buzz, not even hippies. I

89

got things I got to talk over with my grandpa and the patrons.

I smile and wave and double-thumbs-up, bless the group, and go out walkin' again. This time, straight down the road into the desert. I feel buoyant and pulled along by the current of my journey as if I were floating in a river.

I wanted to see stars, but the sky is dark. The fog is in now. My guidebook says it comes in at night and gives all the desert plants a drink.

Alberto's right about inlakesh. We're all different versions of each other: the same soul-substance born in different bodies and families.

That's why literature works. When we read a book, we adopt the point of view of the narrator, who is, so to speak, another I, another oneself.

Hence, the events of this book might as well be happening to *you;* in fact, in the larger sense, we're not separate individuals, but biologically-connected branches of a single entity, the four-dimensional family tree of humanity—which sounds metaphorical, but looks impressive when you see it, life-sized and pulsating, in a full-blown vision, as I would four years later.

This is all by way of saying we're about to switch to second person narration until the end of this chapter. Heads up! It's going to feel weird at first—"you do this, you do that," when *you're* not doing any of it, just reading it or listening to it. But let's just imagine that each of us is a sense organ reporting to the collective brain of a larger self that we all belong to—the species.

So here's what happens, cave salamanders and giant brains aside. It's like this:

Not *my* but *your* sneakers crunch gravel. *Crunch … crunch … crunch … crunch.…*

The fog is in, giving the plants their drink. The world is dim. The stones on the road dart like mice, though the effect isn't strong. *Crunch ... crunch ... crunch ... crunch....*

You run your fingers through your dusty hair again.

You want stronger visions.

You decide to close your eyes for short distances as you walk.

What will you see?

Grant me a vision, Great Spirit, and the power to heal.

Closing your eyes, you see a soldier's head wrapped in barbed wire.

Crunch ... crunch....

Tanks rolling over kids.

Crunch ... crunch....

Skulls wreathed in flame.

Crunch ... crunch....

Boneyards overflowing with unquiet dead.

Crunch ... crunch....

Nightmares you can't unsee, because at some level they're real.

Crunch ... crunch....

Nightmares that never stop.

Crunch ... crunch....

The solution comes to you:

Don't walk with your eyes closed, idiot.

You open them. The visions vanish. The night is velvet-soft.

Crunch ... crunch....

You wonder, *Is that what my problem is? Have I been walking with my eyes closed all these years?*

You walk on, open-eyed.

Crunch ... crunch....

You remember what you dreamed the night before: you're walking in this desert, at night, just like this, when you find a tremendous fenced-in corral where a ghostly

91

rancher with a big white moustache tends herds of extinct mammals.

Again, now, no one's here but spirits.

Will they show themselves? you wonder.

You should sit a while.

You sit crosslegged at the roadside, close your eyes, introspect.

You see the glowing yellow edges of a transparent box. Within, several energies are moving, including an orange square, a little red ball, and a yellow bar. But the one that draws your attention is a jagged, neon-blue line. Whenever it strikes one of the invisible walls of the box and slowly rebounds off it, a man's voice speaks a three-syllable word, a different one each time. Each word contains sounds—phonemes—from Spanish, Italian, and Huichol, one after another: in a single word, three languages, whose order varies by word. When the jagged blue line hits a wall backwards, the word is spoken in reverse.

You listen to this singular speech for a long time, knowing you won't remember the words; as clear as they are now, your mind is experiencing too intently to record much. How quietly magnificent the voice is! What is it saying in the invisible yellow box where bright energies dance in darkness?

Voice and vision fade. You get to your feet, brush off jeans and palms, keep trekking into the dark.

A round hole, three meters wide, floating in the air, ahead of and above you, parallel to the ground. A skylight revealing bright color and rushing wind, brilliant in the velvet blackness.

Looking down at you through the portal are a dozen humanoids whose bodies are brilliantly-colored, constantly shifting designs. "Come up and join us," say the dazzling beings.

Would you be able to get back down?

How would you even get up there in the first place? You've been a fool before.

"Not now," you reply. "Maybe later, when I have a guide. Thank you, though!" You wave to them and walk forward, under the hole with its rushing wind and scintillating colors, past it, down the road to the rhythm of gravel crunching under sneakers. *Crunch ... crunch ... crunch....*

You skid to a halt when, ahead in the fog, coyotes break into song. Five or six brilliant voices howl and squeal in Gregorian coordination. It's the most beautiful music possible. Desert dogs don't usually share this level of music with humans. They could be sky spirits, come to earth to overwhelm you with the finest music imaginable.

When the coyotes fall silent, you direct the crunching of your sneakers back toward town. Somewhere, up ahead, consensus reality awaits, with bills, taxes, ice cream sundaes.

Around you, gliding like ice skaters, are meter-high, slender, gray letters, writing un-words across the pages of the night.

You imagine yourself writing this experience down. You replay scenes and lines in your head. You think up phrases to speak directly to the reader.

To all who might one day read or hear this: Here in the haunted desert of Wirikuta, in the third moon of the year nineteen hundred and ninety-three of the Common Era, I ask the Great Spirit to bless you and your loved ones, now and forever.

Back at the Better-Than-Hilton Hotel, everyone's sleeping. You ninja past Señora Sabas' room, then Alberto's, the Italians', and the Mexicans' rooms. Finally, you ease yourself into John's and yours.

You sit on your hard bed in the dark, pry off your dusty red Converse All-Star low-tops, flex your feet, crack your toes, lie back, stretch, scratch your belly, listen to John's quiet breathing, watch the blue dawn seep into the dark white ceiling like watercolor.

You pack your pack and stealth out without waking the Arizonian.

Señora Sabas is up, wrapped in a shawl against the dawn chill. "Everything OK?" she asks.

"Everything excellent," you say. Again, you quietly admire her eyes, the same pale blue as your mother's. You settle your bill, filled with a sudden urge to hug your mother and tell her you love her. Señora Sabas mentions her cheese-making business. You buy a wheel of delicious-smelling, handmade white cheese. She puts it in a plastic bag and ties the bag with that one simple knot you don't know how to untie.

At 7 a.m., you catch the old, slow train that your guidebook says is called El Burro, the donkey. It's nothing fancy, but super-reliable, and lovingly kept by its caretakers. The comfortable, rattly thing is packed with sleepy, good-natured Mexicans. No seats are left. You're offered a sack of corn in the aisle, and you sit on it. You can lean back against a seat, stretch your legs in front of you. You're comfortable. Not tired, but relaxed. A standing man smiles knowingly at you, one connoisseur to another, before openly breaking in half a doorknob-sized peyote button and sharing it with a seated friend.

A sister and brother, about ten and nine, put their jackets over their heads and gently swat each other with the sleeves: they are elephants.

You close your eyes and see yellow spirograph designs, faint but distinct, slowly shifting.

You wonder how many other people on the train are seeing designs of their own.

At this moment, this train through Peyoteland is the most chilled-out train in the world.

94

Your mind drifts back to Mauricio telling you Jews never travel alone, and what you should have said. *Do you see a great crowd of Jews around me? Well, maybe you do. They're my ancestors, Mauricio. A Jew never travels alone, but always in the company of sparks of consciousness, alive and eternal.*

Of course, Mauricio, that's true about everybody! Don't worry about it, man! We're all one! One love!

You pray for the anti-Semite. And the Burro wanders lovingly through the brightening desert with a gentle clatter, while the passengers chatter or doze, lit by swarms of invisible sparks.

At nine, your stomach murmurs, "Dude! Did you forget all about me?"

You rummage in your pack for your wheel of cheese.

It isn't there.

You realize—to your stomach's annoyance—that you left it on top of Señora Sabas's fridge. She's shorter than the fridge, so it'll likely be up there for some time, like Noah's Ark resting atop Mount Ararat, like a Frisbee stuck on a roof.

***

When the train reaches the station in the city of San Luis Potosí at 11 a.m., you're well-rested, though you haven't slept a wink. You wonder what awaits.

Getting off the train, you're approached by a jittery, pale-skinned guy. He says, "Hi, do you speak English?"

"Sure. I'm from Michigan. Where you from?"

"Ohio. I'm Ray."

"Nathan."

"I've never been outside the States before. Can't speak a word of Spanish. I'm traveling with another guy from Ohio. He's gone crazy. Literally insane. Plus, he's

95

always drunk. He was a good friend before we came here. A neighbor. But now I gotta get away. Can you help me cash my travelers checks so I can start heading home by myself?"

"Piece of cake," you say. You go to a bank with Ray and change $100 in checks into pesos. You can't resist chatting up the girls who work behind the counter. It's the mood you're in.

Ray says, "Thanks a million. Look, I'm going to an ice cream shop now to meet another American guy, a missionary. Wanna come?"

"Sure thing."

Greg the missionary makes you think of a slightly warped reflection of yourself: as close as one could get to being you without actually being you. You and he even look similar—tall, green-eyed, with short brown hair, though his is curly. Over sundaes, Greg tells his story. "Born in upstate New York. Got into drugs and alcohol before ... how can I put this ... *finding solace* in a spirituality that includes Martin Buber's books and the Evangelical movement. I've been living in Mexico for a year and a half. I love the adventurous lifestyle, the new language, the feeling I have of being close to God." He pauses and calls out, "*¡Hola, Marta!*" to a woman walking by. She smiles and waves.

"She reminds me," Greg goes on. "One time I was driving our van into Mexico City. She was in the passenger seat. We always had trouble with that van and never had money to fix it. So, I'm driving, we're going down this long, long, straight hill, and suddenly Marta screams, *¡Gregorio! ¡Mire, mire! ¡La llanta!* Look! The tire! I look in front of the van and I see our rear wheel rolling away ahead of us down the highway!"

Generally, you feel Christians have no business going around the world brainwashing people to leave behind their old religions. But Greg is so kind and funny and sincere that when he invites you and Ray to have lunch at the church, you smoothly accept. Hunger might play a role as well.

At a table in the kitchen in the storefront church with Greg and Ray and a gaggle of friendly Mexican women, you feel utterly content. The pork in chocolate-and-chili-pepper *mole* sauce with corn tortillas is a culinary *tour de force,* the gustatory equivalent of the coyotes' singing the night before. "Who made this miracle?" you inquire. No one wants to accept the praise, but one woman looks especially pleased. For the next half hour, you joke with them nonstop in Spanish. You have everyone but Ray in stitches. They're nearly falling off the chairs and tables they're sitting on.

Eventually a clock is looked at. "Would you like to come to the *culto,* the church service?" you and Ray are asked delicately.

Sure. That seems to be the way the current is flowing.

But, sitting in a pew, listening to lugubrious testimonials of dissolute alcoholics who have found Jesus and promote him to others as if he were a hair care product in a pyramid scheme, you start to tire.

The service presses on, sixty minutes, seventy, eighty minutes, saved sinner after saved sinner. Suddenly it ends, and releases you, like a fist unclenching. Now you can head to the bus station, en route to Guadalajara, Mexico City, Quito, and the jungle.

Outside the storefront church, Greg presents you with a copy of the New Testament in Spanish, a little one with a green plastic cover and the Psalms and Proverbs included. You say goodbye to everyone, wish Ray luck in getting home, and saunter away.

But even when you haven't been melding minds with Grandpa Peyote, you have a poor sense of direction, and now, forget it, so a few minutes later you have to stop to ask the way to the bus station. A simple question to two workers on a street corner blossoms into a forty-minute discussion on the character of Job in the Bible and the question of free will versus predestination. One guy gives you his address so you can look him up next time you're in town. He also sketches you a peyote-proof map to the bus station.

As you walk away, finally oriented, it dawns on you that you'll have to scrap your old ideas about intelligence. You've always believed there's a scale where some people are smarter and some people are dumber. Intellectuals like your family are up at the top, and on down the line to manual laborers and people who do badly in school. But your Mexico trip has been indicating to you that finding people's intelligence is a matter of being able to communicate with them. In other words, if someone seems stupid, it's only because you can't relate to them. Their mind is functioning as well as yours is, it's just processing different information. A phrase from Walt Whitman comes back to you: "Go freely with powerful uneducated persons."

As you stroll under the intelligent-looking late afternoon sky with the map in your hand, the world seems a wiser place.

At the station, a sharply-dressed, dignified rancher in his fifties—the kind that have gray moustaches and enjoy Mariachi music—says, "Where are you coming from?"

"From Real de Catorce."

"Ah, *el peyotito*."

"Yes, the peyotito. Do you know it too?"

98

"Yes. We have great respect for that. It's very useful if one wants to know oneself and the world around. The education we get in schools is beneficial but superficial. There are deeper traditions rooted in this land that go back to the time before the Spanish conquest." The two of you discuss the matter at length.

The bus for Guadalajara pulls out, with you on it. You open the little green Bible that Greg gave you to a random page: Psalm 49. You read, "Why need I fear when evil times come? Only my own sins can ensnare me." Words to savor and remember.

But you've been awake now for thirty-six hours.

You tuck the Bible in your backpack, thank the Great Spirit, and let your eyes close like old, heavy, leather-bound books.

***

The ride to Guadalajara was long, cramped, and bumpy. After you reached the home of the family you stayed with, you were wiped out for a whole day, disappointing your hosts, who wanted to hear well-told tales of the adventures of the gringo who wanted to be a shaman.

9. In the Secret Place of Thunder

Two days later, back in the first person, and with the arguably-illusory distinction between reader and writer reestablished, I flew from Mexico City to Quito, Ecuador's high-altitude capital. Slept in a dilapidated working-class hotel near the central bus station. Joined the South American Explorers Club and spent an afternoon reading in its library.

Decided to visit two tribes, the Siona and the Waorani. The Siona, because an anthropologist wrote that their shamans were the best at drinking *yagé*, pronounced ya-HEY—that was their word for ayahuasca.

The anthropologist detailed how the Siona shamans taught by singing visions into the cups of yagé that their apprentices then drank.

The Siona encouraged strong experiences. When the visions came on, their novice drinkers would scream, vomit, and sometimes even shit themselves in their hammocks as they strove for the highest, strongest visions.

It sounded intense. I wanted intense.

I decided to visit the Waorani (singular: Wao) because of Jeremy Carver's story about being taught by one of their shamans, and because they were the wildest tribe around. I wanted to see human life in the most archaic form possible. Maybe that shaman Jeremy told me about—Nenke—would take me on as an apprentice. By his side, I'd turn into a spirit and fly deep into the mindforest.

I read that the Waorani were formerly, and derogatorily, known as "Aucas," meaning "savages." The word is from the Quichua language, spoken by the descendants of the citizens of the old Inca empire. I read that the Waorani eat more monkey than any other group in the world, and visitors to their territory were expected to share in the consumption of this staple food. I resolved to bring plenty of provisions in order to avoid this activity which felt so close to cannibalism.

The Waorani were divided into two groups, I learned as I leaned back in a big red velvet armchair: the standard, semi-civilized Waorani, who numbered about 1200, and a splinter group called the Tagaeri, of whom there were only a few dozen. After a dispute in the late 1960s, the Tagaeri had retreated deep into the forest, where they lived in a state of intermittent aggression with the others.

The Ecuadorian Amazon had been the target of oil exploration and exploitation since the 1940s. The 1980s saw a move to search for oil on land held by the Tagaeri. Oil exploration would lead to violence between them and the oil workers, as it had in other places where the resource extractors had worked Waorani land.

From the Wao perspective, I read, their territory was becoming infested with super-powered demons that ripped up the forest, built infernal huts atop the bones of the dead, ate the fruits of the palm trees the ancestors had planted, fouled the water, drove away game animals with hellish noise, and worse.

A Wao hunter might chuck spears at such demons upon encountering them in the forest—barbed spears made of the chonta palm, the hardest wood in the forest, launched by arms that had trained to kill since toddlerhood. Spears that could bury themselves in a man's guts, knock him down, rip him up.

But the gun was mightier than the spear. I read the following from 1953 by William S. Burroughs in *The Yage Letters:* "On the boat I talked to a man who knows the Ecuador jungle like his own prick. It seems jungle traders periodically raid the Auca ... and carry off women they keep penned up for the purposes of sex.... I have precise

101

instructions for Auca raiding. It's quite simple. You cover both exits of an Auca house and shoot everybody you don't wanna fuck."

Another man who knew the Ecuador jungle at more or less the same level of detail as his own prick was the bishop of the jungle town of Coca, Alejandro Labaka, a Basque, from northern Spain, a seasoned veteran of missionary work with the non-Tagaeri Waorani. He'd walked naked-but-for-a-string in the forest with them, been adopted by a Waorani family, and learned to speak their language. In 1987, he decided to initiate peaceful contact with the Tagaeri in advance of the search for oil. He and a nun, Inés Arango, were dropped off by helicopter at a tiny, remote Tagaeri settlement.

Five days later, the helicopter crew returned as arranged. The settlement had been abandoned by the Tagaeris, and Labaka's and Arango's naked bodies were splayed on the ground, each pierced by ten or twelve three-meter-long spears made of chonta palm.

Before going out there, Labaka had composed a letter that was to be opened in the event of his death. In it, he requested that if the Tagaeri killed him and Arango, there would be no oil exploration in the area. His wish was respected. He and Arango sacrificed their lives to protect their killers. In the photo of him lying dead in Coca, he was gently smiling.

***

From Quito, I flew to a jungle town called Lago Agrio, in search of Sionas. On the flight, I made friends with three Californians—Jim, Samantha, and Randy, all a decade older than me. On the street in the town, redolent with fragrances of fruit, burning garbage, and physical and moral decomposition, we checked into a hotel, then went out looking for a tour company. A suave mestizo approached us. His broad smile showed he was missing his left lateral incisor. "Vicente Hernández, rainforest guide," he said. "You're looking for a tour?"

Samantha said, "No thank you. We want to go with an established agency."

But Hernandez, smiling, talked fast: "I will provide you with maximum comfort and security, as well as an unparalleled knowledge of the local flora and fauna (and of the local indigenous customs, as I am Quichua on my father's side), while we travel by motorized canoe through the national park, where we can observe ibises, monkeys, and dolphins in the daytime, and caimans in the evening, and we will camp under mosquito nets in comfortable huts every night, and my wife will cook and wash dishes for us all." He finally caught the attention of my skeptical companions. A dozen passersby gathered to watch. I told them, "I hope we're almost as interesting as a TV show." They laughed. Foreigners were always entertaining.

I didn't pay close attention to the negotiations. The Californians were bargaining hard. I would settle for whatever they decided on with Vicente, or whoever else they went with. I was moving through the world with the smooth grace—and, granted, the passivity—of that day on peyote in San Luis Potosí. Whatever life presented, I would accept.

Vicente went on, "I will take you to a Secoya shaman who sometimes drinks yagé with tourists." The Secoyas, I'd read, were related to the Sionas. Maybe their shamans were almost as good as the Siona ones. *It's like Huichols and Coras*, I reflected. *Sometimes you get Sionas, sometimes you get Secoyas.* My companions were uninterested in drinking yagé but curious to meet a shaman. I'd read that shamans who drank yagé with tourists weren't particularly reputable. But meeting this Secoya might be a step in the right direction. At least Vicente seemed capable of getting us into the rainforest.

Negotiations moved to Vicente's cement-walled apartment, which he shared with his extremely pretty wife and their three little daughters. All the adults stayed up late, negotiating. The deal in its final form stipulated a five-day tour for $30 per person per day, except it would be $25 for me, and I would do some chores, to be specified by Vicente. With him, Samantha composed a schedule, neatly organized, hour by hour, day by day. Vicente would pick everyone up at 7:00 at the hotel the following morning.

At 8:00 sharp, he appeared with a bright, gap-toothed smile outside the hotel, accompanied by two pickup truck taxis. His wife and daughters and some baggage and a kitchen stove and a tank of gas and crates of food and dishes were in one, while the other was empty, waiting for us and our gear. Up we hopped and off we zoomed. At 9:05, the expedition shoved off in a motorcanoe, riding low in the water, at the entrance to Cuyabeno National Park. The motor roared, then gasped and sputtered. Vicente did machine CPR on it. It came back to life, then cut out again. Vicente fought for its life, occasionally using a long bamboo pole to prod us away from the riverbank. At 9:30, he got the engine running. He turned us around and brought us back and got a different canoe with a working motor. Our schedule was history. I was quietly glad to have it out of the way.

Laden with nine people and their goods, the new canoe rode even lower in the water than the first had, and water leaked in through the seams. My task, then, was to scoop out water, two or three times a minute, with an empty, two-liter Sprite bottle that had been cut into a bucket shape.

104

From time to time I took up my notebook. "A big toucan above us on a limb," I wrote. "High gray cloud cover with blue cracks in it. Bright yellow-white fuzz where the sun is. Just above the notebook, brown water with gray sky reflection speeds past my feet. Blue flash of a morpho butterfly. The sky's clearing up. Primitive sunlight drips from it like magma. Jim lights a cigarette and goofs off. Samantha half-laughs through her nose at him. He whistles, plays with his cigarette. Randy pops his gum and watches the forest. Samantha writes in a journal. Squirrel monkeys appear for a moment.

"The wind from the canoe's motion is soft on my ankles. Cold drops of spray hit the soles of my feet. A half moon in the morning sky like an eggshell made of cloud. Vines like violin notes hang down into the river. Parrots fly overhead squawking. Web-footed tracks in the mud—capybara, world's largest rodent—where we stopped to pee. I find it's impossible to whistle and yawn at the same time."

In the evening, Vicente landed the canoe on the bank of a lagoon and brought everyone to an empty hut. As his wife started preparing dinner, he cut nettles with his machete and used them to whack his back. He said everyone here did it: it relieved sore muscles. I tried it and with a little imagination could feel it working. When night had fallen, and Jim and Randy and Samantha and I had eaten abundantly from Vicente's wife's decent cooking as their three daughters lounged on our laps chattering about princesses and bunnies, Vicente brought us all outside and down to the water to look for the caimans. He shone a light out into the darkness. "Can you see the reflections of eyes?" He grunted to call them nearer, sounding like he was trying to squeeze out a log. Slowly, the beasts drifted toward us like boats, pairs of gleams peering at the light. He kept grunting. I imitated his grunts. He muttered,

105

"You sound like you're trying to shit." "So do you," I said. Later, when I lay down to sleep, the black water in my mind rocked with the movement of hundred-foot-long swimming reptiles.

***

On the second day, the expedition went further into the park. As the sun built a nest of gold in my brown hair and laid an egg of beauty and inspiration, I hunched over my notebook again. "Vicente caught a huge catfish by leaving a line in the river during the night," I wrote. "His wife is cleaning it now, throwing guts overboard. Their daughters are making string figures.

"Twittering birdcalls through the canopy. Leaves like round, flat hands, with sun shining weakly through.

"I dreamt there was a toll-free number you could call if you had roadkill. The dispatcher would send a vulture.

"Then I invited Lily out on a date, but there were two of her, and they got jealous of each other.

"When I woke in the night, Samantha was growling in her sleep.

"Off goes the motor, and on goes the sweet song of rippling water and far birdcalls and the psychic vibrations of cicadas. A glimpse of blue sky. Trees reach far out over the river for light. Other trees overreach themselves or are undermined by the river and end up in the drink.

"Randy says, 'It's 1993. Why can't they invent a silent engine?'

"Traveling again. Jim was briefly stuck in deep mud after a crap. Macaws squawking wildly, lazily, in the trees behind us. Vines trailing in the water. Other vines not quite there. Samantha cracks her knuckles, whistles a

106

couple of notes, goes back to writing. A blue-green dragonfly speeds alongside the boat. Samantha translates for me the Italian proverb on her notebook: 'To travel gently is to travel safely.'

"We pass through the shadow of a tremendous buttress-rooted *ceiba*—the biggest tree in the forest, Vicente says.

"The sun swings to the left and right behind us as we round a curve. Cloud blurs the shadow of my hand on the page. The shadow of my hand appears and disappears as if I myself were appearing and disappearing. Three distinct levels of cloud are above us now; and between them, beyond them, outer space is thronged with imperceptible intelligences.

"Leaves glistening with water. Water glistening.

"Clouds full of Chinese dragons coiling and uncurling in slow motion.

"The sun licks me suddenly, ferociously; hotly rubs its white fur against my skin. Samantha smears the whiteness of sunblock on her smooth brown legs, and the low clouds are flying, flying."

***

On the third day of the tour, it dawned on me that the only shaman who was likely to drink yagé with me was one who would drink with tourists, because, *de facto,* like it or not, I was a tourist.

On the fourth day, we saw river dolphins in a lagoon, which may have been an omen of some kind.

On the fifth day, the canoe droned out of Cuyabeno National Park and onto the Aguarico River. A few hours upriver, Vicente turned to the left bank and cut the motor. We ground to a halt in the sand. A short, steep trail led to higher ground. Up there, Vicente said, lived don Joaquín Piaguaje, the last Secoya shaman.

Our guide emitted a loud, long *Hoooooooooooooooooooo!*, then sprang out of the canoe and dragged it higher up onto the small beach. He sank the bamboo pole into the damp sand, leaned in to push the pole deep, tied the canoe to the pole.

Atop the embankment, there came a frenzied barking from two skinny hunting dogs, one white and tan, the other black. Soon the shaman himself appeared, barrel-chested, wearing a purple tunic that came down to his shins. Indignantly, in his own language, he ordered the dogs to shut up—an order with which they struggled to comply. The man had a short, military-style haircut, and looked, I thought, Tibetan, with small eyes, high cheekbones, and broad nose. He exchanged a few words with Vicente, drove the dogs away with a gesture (they snorted and trotted away, satisfied), and invited everyone up, flashing a grin that was missing a left central incisor.

Leaving the baggage in the canoe, the rest of us scrambled ashore. We went up a steep path to a flat patio of dirt, then up a stairway made of a pair of notched logs, into a hut, which was on posts, two meters off the ground. Don Joaquín introduced his wife, Maribel, a plump woman with very long, wavy black hair and a brilliant smile. We all sat crosslegged on a firm, yielding floor that, Vicente noted, was made of split palm wood. The roof of the hut, I saw, was made of overlapping palm fronds lashed to poles which in turn were supported by beams. Maribel opened an aluminum pot full of mashed, boiled, ripe, yellow plantain, and spooned some of it out into aluminum bowls, added water to each and mixed well, and handed one to each guest.

Joaquín and Vicente caught up on news of mutual acquaintances. I became immersed in the chewy sweetness

108

of the plantain drink. Joaquín sounded intelligent and
accessible. Curiously, his eyebrows seemed to have been
shaven off. After the drinks, he showed us around the
garden of plantain and banana plants, like four-meter-tall
frozen fountains of green water, and the patch of
modestly-sized *yuca* plants (there's an edible part that
grows underground, Vicente said) with leaves shaped like
hands.

I trailed behind the shaman's swaying back
underneath the arching leaves, and thought I might want
to follow him down his path for a while.

Up in the hut again, my companions examined
necklaces and bracelets that Maribel was offering for sale,
made with local seeds. I mustered my courage and
addressed the shaman. "Don Joaquín, I hear you
sometimes drink yagé with tourists. Would you do that
with me?"

He replied in a Spanish that was strongly accented,
precisely enunciated, and slightly distorted. "It's fine," he
said. "You going downriver to the village and staying with
my relatives there for two nights. Coming back on Sunday
morning and we drinking Sunday night."

The sound of an engine announced a canoe
heading downriver. Vicente hailed the motorist, a Secoya,
who agreed to give me a ride to the village. I transferred
my pack and said goodbye to everyone and was soon
underway.

The motorist—a placid, smooth-faced man—
shook my hand and introduced himself over the noise of
the motor: "Gervasio Piaguaje. I'm Joaquín's daughter-in-
law's brother. You can stay in my house. Can you help me
pronounce English? I'm starting a tourism business with
some guys from Quito and studying an English textbook.
Would you tape-record yourself reading it out loud?"

"Sure. What's the name of this village where we're going?"

"Siecoya."

"Like Secoya, the tribe."

"Yes, but *Si*ecoya."

"What does it mean?"

"It means another Siecoya, in another place. A place where we came from."

He steered the canoe to land on the right bank, alongside five other dugouts. He tied it with a long rope to a root sticking out of the eroded bank, then came back and steadied it so I could jump out with my pack. He climbed on board again to remove the 45-horsepower Yamaha motor, which must have weighed two hundred pounds. He easily shouldered the machine and, barefoot, led the way to the village. I could see a dozen huts and a school. "There are other houses in the forest," he noted.

He brought me to a two-story wooden house. His three kids ran out and greeted him. He set the motor on the ground with an *Uff!* and a smile. His wife appeared in the doorway and he briefed her. She smiled and nodded, and the two of them showed me where I could put my pack and where I could sleep, on the second floor near a shelf on which rested Gervasio's English textbook and a moldy Bible in Spanish. *They don't yet know how to take care of books*, I thought.

After dinner, Gervasio told me about the Secoyas' community here on the Aguarico River and about their language. The group had migrated from territory that now belongs to Peru. At the end of the 1930s, they were enslaved to a man who made them tap rubber for him. During a war between Peru and Ecuador that lasted from 1940 to 1941, they escaped. They made their way to Cuyabeno, a week's journey through the forest. In 1959, a missionary couple from the United States contacted them

110

there, lived with them, and started christianizing them. This led to the gradual disappearance of the yagé ceremony. In 1973, the group migrated up the Aguarico to their present location. As Gervasio spoke, I remembered the dolphin skeleton cloud I'd seen in the sky above my college, and my certainty that I'd been invited to the forest by shamans active around the time of my conception. The dates matched up, roughly. Still, as with so much of my story, there was no way to know if it was a fantasy or not.

I took notes on Gervasio's lesson on Paicoca, the Secoyas' language:

It has twelve vowels: a, e, i, o, u, ë, a̠, e̠, i̠, o̠, u̠, ë̠. The underlined ones are nasal. The language is written with a Spanish-based system, so, for example, the letter ñ is used for the sound "ny," and the letter j is used for the sound of an English h.

Ao̠: white flatbread made of yuca, the plant with hand-shaped leaves that Joaquín and Maribel have. Ao̠ is slightly sour and very hard when eaten dry. Gervasio's wife fed me ao̠ with soup, and in the broth it softened immediately. Yuca is a root vegetable, starchy like a potato, but large, long and white, with a thick skin that's chopped and pried off before the yuca is boiled.

Yai: jaguar.

Siaya: river.

Wai: meat.

Siaya wai: fish.

Jai siaya, or Jaiya: big river—the Aguarico. Pronounced Haiya.

Pai̠: people. The "p" is close to a "b," and the "i" is nasal, so it could also be written "bai," "pain," or "bain." In English orthography it would be something like "pine" or "bine" with the n only half-pronounced—halfway to "pie" or "buy."

Paicoca: the peoples' speech.

111

Airo pai: forest people. Po pai, white people. Nea pai, black people. Po pai ke, you're a white guy.

Piaguaje, a family name: pia, little bird; guaje, pronounced like wahey, and meaning fresh, young, green. Payaguaje, the other major Secoya family name: paya, oil on the skin of the face. They had that name because people said they were strong shamans, and in the ceremony, their faces would become oily, a sign of their power.

Ñata wahë (or guaje): good morning—literally, "Morning fresh?"

Kwepe: insane, or under the influence of yagé. (Brain-fried, as my mom would say.)

Hn-hn: yes. It could be spelled jn-jn because of the Spanish orthography. (Consistency is the hobgoblin of small minds.) It sounds like the English affirmation "hm-hm" with the m's replaced with n's. The stress is on the second hn.

Pani: no.

Yuuri: now.

Deóhi: thank you.

Uncucui: yagé drinker.

Paihuhu: healer.

***

Over the next few days, I coached Gervasio on English and played soccer with his son. On Sunday morning, I skipped breakfast so I could fast all day, as instructed, and my host delivered me to Joaquín's place. The uncucui was in the middle of chopping firewood to cook the brew. He wouldn't accept my help. Then, with a machete, he cut a two-meter-long, wrist-thick section of a yagé vine that was growing on a pair of tall trees behind his house. He chopped the vine into sections, then

112

pounded it with a hand-carved wooden mallet so the bark came off and the vine sections opened up a little. They turned from yellow-brown to orange as they oxidized in the air. He boiled them in a huge aluminum pot together with leaves he gathered from another vine that he called *yagé ocó,* water yagé.

A neighbor from across the river stopped by and Joaquín arranged for me to catch a ride with him out of Secoya territory the following morning.

We talked all day. Joaquín's Spanish was idiosyncratic, heavy on gerunds—the well-worn imperfections of someone who had spoken ungrammatically for over half a century. He said his parents had both died when he was very small and his grandparents raised him. His grandfather gave him yagé when he was a boy. He wept and had visions for three days and nights. "It's very important, crying," he said, tipping his head back, looking at me. "Getting everything out."

"What did you see in the visions?"

"All kinds of spirits coming from the forest and the sky. Jaguars! Mirrors! People riding on the backs of giant snakes!" Grinning, he mimed these things with his hand. "So many visions! How could I tell you them all? And so clear, like television!"

"I've taken things that are like yagé," I said. "LSD—that's a chemical—and mushrooms. I liked them but I didn't want to do them in the city. Up in Mexico I had a cactus called peyote and that was great. I heard wild dogs called coyotes singing, and saw beautiful, radiant people in the sky who were all different colors."

"A usted le gusta chumar," the shaman commented. *"Usted será un buen hombre."* You like to trip. You'll be a good man.

113

I knew the verb "chumar" from my reading, but this was the first time I'd heard it used. It was derived from the name of an Andean hallucinogen, the San Pedro cactus, known to the indigenous people as *achuma*. *"A usted le gusta chumar,"* I repeated to myself. To you it pleases to choom. The word is onomatopoeic, like peyote. A sound effect from a comic book as someone plunges into the astral plane: *CHOOM!*

Joaquín's words lightened my heart, and not just because of the verb.

I said, "Thank you. I'm fed up with feeling like a criminal for wanting to trip in the United States."

He said, "Our Secoya culture here, old times, the best men were the best yagé drinkers. If a man not staying up all night drinking and chanting for the good of the tribe, lazy and useless."

"Ah."

"Even so," he went on, "people sometimes persecuting shamans. There was a shaman. Some accusing him of witchcraft, because people getting sick and dying. In fact, he doing all he could to save lives, to drive off the evil that was attacking his community. But because he was powerful, some within the community suspecting him, preparing to kill him. Then one day, some other people paddling down out of the sky in canoes."

"Some people paddled down out of the sky in canoes?" I echoed.

"That's right. They paddling canoes in the sky, paddling down and landing on the earth. The shaman getting into one of those canoes. Then they paddling back up into the sky, taking him away with them. The people on the earth never seeing the shaman again. The disease continuing to kill people, and the people on the earth realizing they were wrong, it wasn't him."

114

"I see," I said. "He went off with those people into another world."

"That's right."

"A higher world."

"Right. The sky. We calling that world *ma'temo*. The people who live there, *ma'temo pai.*"

"The objection to hallucinogens where I come from," I said, "is that they could cause brain damage or insanity. But the objection to hallucinogens here is that they might make the user powerful and evil."

"That's how it is."

The sun was setting. The last light of the day grazed the treetops, gold on green. Joaquín plucked from a bush a spiky, green seedpod and opened it with his fingers. *Achiote,* he said it was called. An oily, bright red juice coated the seeds inside. The shaman broke off a long, thin sliver of palm wood from one of the posts of the hut, rubbed it in the juice, and on my forehead and cheeks, and on his own, printed diagonal lines and asterisks. He remarked, "This meaning we're children of the sky."

He said we'd be silent for an hour before drinking. We rested, he in an old hammock, I on a low wooden stool. On the other side of the hut, Maribel and their little granddaughter Xiomara hung a big mosquito net over some mats and blankets and lay down to sleep.

Though I was close to my goal of trying ayahuasca, my heart was heavy. In the past, all the men in the village would have assembled to drink. Now it was just one old guy and a tourist. The missionaries had won. The tradition was dead. The Secoyas were a bust. Maybe I could find Sionas later.

After a dark, quiet hour, Joaquín lit a kerosene lamp—a simple one, lacking a round glass wall around its flame, which danced in the gentle breeze. My host filled a blue plastic mug with the brown brew and chanted over it.

115

I'd never heard anything like that chant. Wobbly was the word for it, wobbly like a canoe on the river, like a hammock, like the wobbly flame that dimly lit the inside of the hut.

Having chanted, the uncucui drank, rinsed his mouth with water from a red plastic mug, refilled the blue cup, chanted over it, handed it to me.

The moment had come. The awful liquid I was choking down was as bitter as the peyote had been, and more nauseating. *The taste of visions?* I wondered, rinsing out my mouth with water and spitting the water, as my host had done, into a crack between the floorboards. I lay back, listening to the invisible insect musicians that illuminated the dark night outside.

Forty minutes passed.

Joaquín picked up a kind of fan made of a bundle of spearhead-shaped leaves, and shook it in rhythm to his wobbly chanting.

He broke off and growled like a jaguar.

The back of my neck prickled. He resumed singing. The growl had seemed natural, unself-conscious. Bizarre. Any time I'd heard someone imitate an animal, it had sounded contrived.

He fell silent, then said, "Feeling the yagé?"

"No."

"Wanting another cup?"

"Please."

Half an hour later, wondering if I'm going to "choom," I glanced up at the palm-frond ceiling. By the light of the kerosene lamp, the ceiling is vibrating. So am I. As Nezahualcoyotl implied it would, the illusion of solidity dissolves, and I see how everything is made of waves. I try to speak, but can only sing, in Spanish, *"Este es el alucinógeno más fuerte que he tomado,"* this is the strongest hallucinogen I've ever taken.

116

Earlier I felt sad that there were only the two of us. Now the night is buzzing with consciousness. It's as if every thought every being has ever had here trembles in the air. The fact that only two human bodies are present is irrelevant. Joaquín's voice seems thousands chanting.

Nausea hits—a warning sign, an exclamation point. "I have to vomit," I mutter. Earlier, Joaquín said I could puke off the side of the hut if I needed to. Now, though, he sits up in his old hammock and snaps, "Don't vomit! Keep it down!"

"I can't," I groan, and make for the edge of the hut, and crouch there, breathing deeply, balancing on the balls of my feet, seething with a thunderous energy.

"Don't fall," urges the old man behind me. "Don't fall."

A voice much deeper than my ordinary one responds, "Sometimes the human doesn't fall."

A tremendous force surges from the tip of my tailbone up my spine to spew with the yagé out my mouth. As I expel the bitter liquid and the energy like a throatful of embers into the darkness, my body emits a deep, choking groan. Another surge of the nausea brings up more yagé and a fiery gleam that I roar with, louder and clearer now with the sign of victory. Another convulsion of my stomach and I'm empty, pure, fantastically energized. I roar and roar and roar in defiance of everything that has ever sullied my soul.

A commotion behind me. Under the hut, the two dogs are barking at me, alarmed about the large mammal roaring up here. Joaquín and Maribel are shushing them. Not shushing me, because, as I read at the Explorers Club, it's expected that novice drinkers will make a lot of noise, but the dogs. I pause and say to the dogs in a normal tone of voice, in English, "Be quiet, it's just a human acting

117

crazy on yagé." They immediately fall silent, and I resume roaring, undisturbed.

Later, I stand, and make my way back, and put a questioning hand on the rope of Joaquín's old hammock. The uncucui makes room for me. I recline next to him, facing the other way. Separated by a taut fold of net-like palm fiber mesh, our left hips pressed together, we take turns singing. Inspiring and responding to my thoughts, his wobbly songs are among the most beautiful sounds I've ever heard, up there with the coyotes in Wirikuta. For my part, I sing "Wavy wavy wavy wavy wavy" to a simple tune, chant "Hey-ya-hey-ya" and decide "yagé" is onomatopoeic, ask "Oh, really?" in a dozen different ways, cooing it, growling it, shouting it like a come-cry. Then, surrounded by and filled with thunder, I boom at the top of my lungs. The spirit of thunder is visiting, celebrating, bellowing through a human body. When this happened to the Vikings, they called it Thor. He's here. *Greetings, my lord. Blessings and explosions.*

Later, I rave spontaneous neologisms, thinking, *Why settle for words that have already been spoken? Our nature is to create language, not just repeat it.*

In yagé, I go on, *I've found my life's work. I'll report on this, I'll analyze it, I'll let others contemplate through the lens of my experience this profound natural magic.*

During hours of trance and song, Joaquín and I establish a telepathic bond. Wordlessly, we agree to work together as teacher and student. Our minds meld like two bubbles joining at the surface of water, or like two candle flames that become one when held together.

Deep in the night, interspersing falsetto squeals with guttural growls, wriggling too hard, I inadvertantly snap some of the worn-out palm fiber strings on my side of the old hammock, and fall through nearly to the floor. I'm just holding myself in by my elbows.

Fuck. I've destroyed this hammock. I can't be trusted with people's things.

Worse, it's not just me, it's everyone. When we enjoy ourselves too much, we lose control. Gays get AIDS from having too much fun without protection. Uncle Pat drank too much and died in a car crash. Humanity itself is dying of its own excesses.

With a heavy sigh, my ass inches from the floor, I silently swear to be cautious and never too happy.

Joaquín's voice, compassionate, reaches me like a lifeline: *"Aguántalo, aguántalo."* Deal with it, don't let it get you down.

Dealing with it as best I can, I clamber out of the broken hammock, wrap a blanket around myself, and fall asleep on the floor.

***

Over breakfast, I wondered if there had really been a telepathic bond. Cautiously, I said, "You know, I have this plan to visit the Waoranis south of here, but I'd almost rather stay around here and study with you."

Without skipping a beat, Joaquín replied, "You wanting to study with me, coming back another year, staying two months, bringing me multicolored glass beads and a trunk that locks for me to keep my clothes in."

The neighbor's outboard motor was growling in the river below. We'd never discussed a price for the ceremony. How could you put a price on something like that? I took out my wallet and handed Joaquín a wad of bills without counting it; he accepted it and put it away without counting it. Then I didn't see him again for eighteen months.

10. The Wildest Ones

I made my way to the jungle town of Coca, where Bishop Labaka had lived and from where he had gone out to die. Coca was an oil town, muddy and messy. I got in after dark, checked into the Hotel Auca, and dined on greasy chicken and rice in a restaurant next door. The only other guests were a loud-voiced, sloppy-drunk Texan in his seventies; a pretty teenaged hooker, around whose graceful neck the old man hung like a deranged albatross; and a pimp or guardian, about twenty. The girl and boy flashed me embarrassed smiles. The Texan wasn't even aware I was there. The young Ecuadorians tended their cash cow gently.

Up early next morning, I saw two indigenous guys conversing on the street. They had bad teeth, so I thought they might be Waorani, because Waorani wouldn't have dental care. I said, "Excuse me, are you guys Waorani?"

The older, shorter one responded, "Yes."

"I'd like to go into your territory to do some tourism. Could you take me?"

They conferred in a language that sounded like thick rubber bands being strummed, and the same man responded, "Yes."

"I'd like to visit a shaman. Would that be possible?"

More discussion, then, "Yes."

"I'd like to go for three weeks. I could offer you 500,000 sucres in cash up front for everything: food, transportation, lodging. Is that OK?" At 2000 sucres to a dollar, the offer came to $250.

More discussion. "It's OK."

120

I asked their names. The older, shorter one was Obe; his taller, younger companion, Camilo. They didn't seem interested in what my name was.

We met at the market the next morning and used part of the money to buy three weeks' worth of supplies for three men: pineapples, papayas, oranges, rolls, instant milk, instant coffee, rice, spaghetti noodles, onions, carrots, potatoes, flour, sugar, garlic, three kilos of animal crackers, two bottles of ketchup, ten cans of tuna, five cans of mackerel, two bottles of vegetable oil, soap for dishes, soap for clothes.

Separately, I bought a pair of rubber boots. The market stalls only sold them up to size 43, and my feet were a few sizes bigger. Fortunately, we wouldn't be hiking much, just riding in a canoe.

The Waorani territory was in a national park, or vice-versa. Before leaving Coca, Obe and Camilo registered my visit with the police, but not with the park authorities, because they had no guiding papers, and on that level, it was forbidden for them to bring me in.

We rode an open-sided bus called a *ranchera* to an abandoned oil drilling camp. A Waorani village now occupied the site. As we arrived, men and women were working with shovels and machetes, digging up old plastic tarps out of the ground to cut up and make into hammocks. In the shadow of a wooden hut, women were searching each other's heads for lice and eating them. Obe and Camilo gave away some of our food to relatives of theirs. Recalling my smooth, calm peyote vibe, I didn't say anything, sure they wouldn't let me go hungry. Then Obe came up and said, "I need another 20,000 sucres to buy fishhooks."

My face flushed. I said, "No! Take it out of the cash I paid you in Coca."

Expressionless, he nodded and padded away.

A Wao named Miguel, who owned an aluminum motorboat, was enlisted to pick me up downriver. I said, "In three weeks."

Miguel said, "Huh?"

"Three weeks."

He looked at me blankly.

A calendar had been nailed up on the wall of a hut. It displayed the correct month, March, 1993. I said, "This is today. This is tomorrow. This is the day after. Down here..." (I flipped to April) "is three weeks from now. Please pick me up then."

Without conviction, he nodded.

My guides and I slept on a sleeping platform made of boards in the home of some relatives.

Next morning, we headed downriver in a canoe, Obe in front, I in the middle, Camilo in back. There was a motor, but they didn't use it, just guided the craft with paddles—saving the gas for the return journey upriver.

Rounding a bend, we saw turtles sunning themselves on a log. Obe and Camilo instantly whipped their paddles down to smack the water with a *CRACK!* As one, the reptiles slid into the river into the river. My guides cackled and whooped.

What the frickity frick? I thought. *They make fun of turtles?*

When the canoe traveled close to a riverbank where trees reached out over the water, Obe held branches out of his way and released them to snap them back in my face, then laughed. He seemed to despise me. Camilo, though, was easygoing and friendly. I felt I could trust him a hundred percent.

It was sunny, so I slathered on sunblock. That attracted mosquitoes, so I squirted on insect repellent. Sweat squeezed out of my pores and ran down my greasy skin. The Amazonian mosquitoes dive-bombed me, more

122

drawn to my blood than repelled by N,N-Diethyl-meta-toluamide. In addition to their devil-may-care attitude toward the chemical, they were much faster than their northern cousins. I was unable to kill more than one or two, while they scored hit after hit on my back and legs.

At noon, black clouds filled the sky. I covered my backpack with plastic bags. Rain came slamming down, rinsing the slime off my skin. I used a cut-down Fanta bottle to bail the canoe. After two hours, the rain ended, and we had four more hours of sun, sunblock, mosquitos, and mosquito repellent.

I read from James Joyce's jungly novel *Finnegans Wake,* muttering it aloud to help me focus. It made little sense, but reading put me inside a psychological force field, and its glossolalic neologisms reconnected me to the night of yagé.

At dusk, we reached another village. As the people came toward us calling greetings, Obe hauled the prow of the canoe out of the water, tied it up, blew his nose between his hands, and wiped the snot on the trunk of a tree. (I thought, *How long since my ancestors did that?*) In the village, Obe and Camilo gave more food away, then made dinner for themselves and me. They set up a tent for us three to sleep in and tied its nylon strings to nearby trees using secure, single-loop, easily-untieable knots like half of a shoelace knot.

***

In the morning fog, the village kids were delighted to have a pale, hairy giant in their midst. Laughing, they grabbed my fingers and pulled me this way and that, like a helium balloon, showing me the pet parrots, the skinny hunting dogs, the baby monkey, the pineapple plants on which fruits were beginning to develop, the rope swing

123

over the river. I felt a pang of envy. They had the important things: people and nature. No cars, no pollution, no stress. I remembered an ecologist's argument that progress had actually made human life worse. *What've we gained?* I mulled as the giggling kids tugged me across the damp grass. *Bigger and more complex structures in politics, economics, architecture, engineering, science.... Maybe one individual isn't capable of knowing more than another individual, but one society can possess more total knowledge, distributed among its members.*

When I packed my gear, a bar of bath soap and a King Crimson cassette tape were missing. (In political terms, they had been *socialized*, or perhaps *nationalized*. As a leftist, I had to accept this.)

We set out on the river. My guides split their sides laughing at turtles they scared off logs. And that sun blazed, and those mosquitos zipped away with our blood. Then raindrops blasted down like cuss words from God. Then came another whine of tiny wings, and our skins were drilled like oilfields as the sun blazed again like a campfire in the sky without even a rainbow for thanks.

I recalled Nezahualcoyotl's vision of the sun turning blue and exploding, and my own that the sun was composed of happy, communalistic spirits working together to generate heat and light. Now the flaming thing was like a 1940s cop clubbing me with a nightstick.

Satiated, the cloud of mosquitoes let itself be blown by the breeze into the forest. The eye of the day roasted me. I lay back and put *Finnegans Wake* over my face, creating a Shroud of Turin effect on pages 290 and 291 with my sunblock. I felt something tickle the back of my hand. Two butterflies, black, orange, and clear, were sipping my sweat with their curly tongues.

At dusk we reached another village. Obe and Camilo doled out nearly all the remaining supplies. I got out my beard trimmer and trimmed my face fur. Obe and a couple of local guys came over to watch. When I was done, Obe took the machine from me. I showed him how it worked. He grabbed a boy who was walking by, and, grinning, shaved a broad line up the back of his head. Delighted, the men laughed. The boy was unfazed.

The next morning I saw that we three had no provisions for the next two and a half weeks but a mostly-full jar of instant coffee, one and a half kilos of spaghetti noodles, a mostly-full bottle of ketchup, and a few onions whose outer layers were beginning to rot. I wasn't completely surprised. I'd read that the Waorani share their food and their few possessions. I wasn't terribly worried; I figured they'd feed us somehow, though I hoped it wouldn't be with monkeys. The thing I was most possessive of was what I figured the Waorani wouldn't want to steal—I mean, socialize: my pump-action water purifier. Since Cuyabeno, when I was in the jungle, I'd pumped all my drinking water through it. *I don't want to get parasites,* I mulled. *If I have to share my food, I want to share it with folks outside me, not inside.* I was interrupted in this train of thought by Obe asking, expressionless, "What do you want for breakfast?"

Like there's a choice, I thought, and snapped, "Coffee, spaghetti, ketchup, and onions." The Wao nodded and prepared it. He, Camilo, and I ate, then headed out on the river again. Maybe I should have given him more money for fishhooks.

Hours later, after the rain had stopped, Camilo blurted something to Obe and raised his muzzle-loading shotgun and fired toward the riverbank. I heard a tumbling-down in the trees. My guides beached the canoe and went and fetched two dead woolly monkeys, a mother and her baby, the size of a big cat and its kitten. The black-furred monkeys had jet black skin. Their long, strong tails

125

were mostly furred, except for a long pad of black skin on the last third of the underside, which they would use to grip branches they hung from.

Back on the river, I was idly looking at these tails when the baby monkey twitched: it was still alive. I flashed back to a childhood memory. Walking down a sidewalk, my dad and I had seen a beetle whose abdomen had been stepped on. The insect was stuck to the sidewalk by its own gore, and uselessly scrabbled with its legs. My dad murmured, "Poor thing; I'll put it out of its misery," and mercifully flattened it with a stomp of his soft brown shoe. Now I knew I had to end the baby monkey's suffering. "I have to kill it," I said to my companions. I picked the animal up by its back and halfheartedly hit it on the head with the blunt side of an axe. It gave a dull snarl. I started to choke it but couldn't stand to imagine the tactile sensation of doing that. Obe, puzzled but going with the flow, handed me a piece of twine. I wrapped it around the animal's neck but didn't have the heart to tighten it. My guides talked to each other, baffled. Willing its soul to its mother, I held the animal underwater off the side of the canoe. It struggled like mad and then finally expired. I took it out and handed it to Obe, who tossed it into the bottom of the canoe beside its mother. (Years later, I figured out it'd only been stunned by the fall and would've been fine if I hadn't killed it.) I felt awful. Jennifer's face flashed into my mind, and I thought again of a fetus that could have been my child. Trembling, I picked up *Finnegans Wake* again and got busy muttering its incomprehensible language, trying to ignore the psychological demons buzzing inside my head.

Soon we heard the noise of an engine. A canoe appeared. It was the only traffic we'd encountered heading upriver. In it were ten Waorani, who immediately started talking with Obe and Camilo. There was also a white guy

126

in his 30s, muscular, bald and tattooed, with earrings all up both ears and, I saw when we started talking, green irises with black flecks in them. "Andy Johnson from Toronto," he said, shaking my hand hard across the water between our canoes. "I started here as a tourist and turned into a guide. Not really sure how that happened! Been in and out of Waorani territory for ten years. I was just in one of their villages for a month without seeing anyone but Waoranis. Actually, I'm furious at these guys. Yesterday they killed a harpy eagle. The largest Amazonian bird of prey. Beautiful, majestic animal. These bastards broke its wing and chopped off its feet so they could watch it hop around as it died. They thought that was the funniest thing they'd ever seen."

"That's insane."

"I tried to stop them but they just laughed at me. They're sadists."

"These guys I'm riding with, every time they round a bend and there are turtles sunning themselves on a log, they slap their paddles on the water to scare them, and they laugh like crazy!"

"Yup. That's Waoranis for you. Totally. I love 'em, but, damn!"

"Also, they shot these monkeys. I had to kill the baby to put it out of its misery."

"Well, the Waoranis eat monkey. If you want to hang with them, you gotta cope with eating what they eat."

"Well, I'm not here to pursue a bourgeois North American lifestyle, you know? But that's fucked up. I mean, I understand it, but...."

"So why *are* you here?"

"I heard about the Waoranis from a guy I met up in the States. I wanted to see how people live in, like, a primitive state, before their whole lifestyle disappears. The

127

guy I met told me he'd hung out with a shaman called Nenke."

"Really? This is Nenke right here." Andy indicated one of the older guys chatting heatedly with Camilo and Obe. The charismatic one, the leader. I stared at him, memorized his Prince Valiant haircut and his feline face. Like the other older Waorani, his ears had been pierced and stretched so the lobes dangled like rubber bands. Actually, he was why I was in this country in the first place. I tried to look at him through the spirit eyes in my chest and tried to attract his attention telepathically, but he acted like I wasn't there.

Andy said, "Who told you about him?"

"Guy named Jeremy Carver."

"Don't know him. Listen, don't get me wrong. I love the Waoranis. They're cruel, but they're also incredibly warm. If they accept you, you're like one of them. And this sadism we're talking about, I think it's in everyone, even though you and I come from societies that try to keep it down. Last year I was in Guatemala City at a market when some people caught a thief. The whole crowd stripped him naked and beat him bloody. And I found myself yelling right along with them."

Andy looked into the forest, then back at me with eyes like green zodiacs. "I think we are all potentially Caligulas."

"Maybe so," I agreed. I'd thought it was just me.

I wondered about cultural faux pas that I might make, endangering my safety. "Are there any taboos I should know about? You know what I mean? Things I shouldn't do?"

Andy shook his head and looked at me evenly. "You can do whatever the fuck you want."

I nodded.

128

"By the way," he remarked, "did you know you're heading into Tagaeri territory?"

"Yeah? I read something about them. They're like wild Waoranis?"

"Yeah, they split off from the rest of the tribe about 30 years ago. It's a little group, nobody knows how many, maybe 40 people. They're at war with the others and they kill anyone who goes into their territory. The stretch of forest that you're heading into is where they live. Ah, that reminds me." The Waorani had been winding up their conversation and the pilot of Andy's canoe yanked the cord that started the outboard motor, which roared to life. The Canadian yelled so I could hear him, "THE LAST TWO TOURISTS WHO WENT DOWN THIS RIVER WERE MURDERED LAST WEEK! NOBODY KNOWS WHO KILLED 'EM! MAYBE THE TAGAERIS! MAYBE THE TAME WAORANIS LIKE THESE GUYS HERE! ANYWAY, THAT'S WHAT THE PEOPLE IN THE VILLAGES ARE SAYING! I THOUGHT YOU SHOULD KNOW!"

I stared at him.

"WELL, HAVE A GOOD TRIP, AND TAKE CARE," the Canadian concluded with a broad grin, waving to me and turning away to face forward into the spray as the two canoes drew apart.

***

At dusk, Camilo and Obe put up the tent and made a fire as usual, dousing the wood in diesel to make it easy to light. I observed them closely, convinced that Camilo was innocent of the double murder but suspicious that Obe might know something about it. The two men roasted the two monkeys, which then smelled horribly of burnt hair and looked like child victims of a terrible fire,

129

each face pulled into a rictus of agony. Soon Camilo was ripping the mother's left arm from her torso and handing it to me. The limb was covered in crisp skin and charred fur. The hand looked like that of a small black person, only the palm was black too and the thumb was flush against the other digits. I gripped the hand and sank my teeth into the arm, tasting the bitter remains of the hair, the tough, oily skin, the thin layer of fat, and the moistness of the meat that was only, to my taste, half-cooked. I hoped it wouldn't give me parasites. I chewed and chewed, wondering if it were possible to bite microorganisms to death. Muscle fibers jammed in between my teeth. I pitched the gnawed bones behind me into the forest. Camilo handed me a leg. "Eat more," he urged with a warm smile. "Eating monkey will make you strong like us." Obe, chewing, nodded in sage agreement. Skeptical, I bit in hard. *If I want to stay in the jungle,* I thought as I masticated, *I have to accept this.*

"I read in Quito that there are 1200 Waorani, including the Tagaeri," I remarked after dinner as we sat around the dying fire.

"That's right," said Camilo. "But in the past, there were many more."

"How many?"

He and Obe conferred for a while, then he answered soberly: "One million." Obe nodded.

I stood up, stretched, saw stars beyond the canopy. "What's the Waorani word for star?" I asked.

"Nemmo," said Camilo.

The two men suddenly started whispering to each other. "Did you hear that?" Camilo asked me.

"No…?"

"Tagaeri!" he hissed. "*Hooo … hooo ….* Talking to each other." I listened closely and dimly heard something that might have been a hoot. "There!" Camilo said.

Camilo got to his feet and began bellowing a diatribe in Waorani. After a few minutes Obe leaned over and reported, "He just told them the government will drop bombs on their village if they hurt us." Camilo fired his shotgun for emphasis. *BOOM!* Then he bellowed some more.

To the sound of Camilo and Obe keeping awake by talking to each other, I prepared to sleep, curling around a machete that wouldn't have done any good against a circle of men armed with three-meter spears. I thought they wouldn't attack, though. The presence of the shotgun meant that one of them would get a face full of buckshot, and there was no countervailing advantage for them in killing us travelers.

Furthermore, I'd gotten into the habit of imagining that my Latin American adventure—and my life itself—was a screenplay, and I thought it unlikely that the writer would kill off the main character so early in the film. I also figured within a couple of years I could complete a real screenplay based on my Latin American adventure, and have it filmed by independent producers. This would be one of the scenes.

I closed my eyes. My guides' voices sounded like rubber bands being strummed. The sounds of the jungle are massive, indecipherable, rich, purple—great flowers with spearmen crouching behind them like wasps. I twitched and shook myself awake again.

I remembered Jeremy Carver dancing with anacondas, and soon I'm dancing with the scaly critters myself. They're swarming up off the river, lighter and lighter, brighter and brighter—and I'm asleep.

***

131

Obe and I are relaxing in a natural hot spring in the jungle with a beautiful Wao woman. Tree roots dangle into the pool. Obe and the woman embrace and kiss, then Obe crouches down and springs out of the pool with a great splash. Dripping, shaking the water off his short black mane, he strides down a path into the forest. The woman turns and wraps her arms around me. We hold our breath and sink underwater and kiss. We rise to the surface, breathe, sink under the water, and make love.

Jubilant to have survived, Camilo and Obe shook me awake at dawn. We paddled downriver in a blur of mosquitoes, rain, turtles, blazing sunshine, muzzle-loading shotguns, and dead monkeys.

Two days and four primate meals later, we stopped at another tiny village. Camilo and Obe talked with the people there. Then we set out again, together with a humble, inquisitive guy nicknamed Pata—a Spanish word meaning the paw of an animal. Obe told me Pata would be my guide for the rest of the tour. Carlos added that Pata was the brother of Manuel, the villager with the boat who was supposed to pick me up in two weeks.

We floated downriver for three hours, then reached our destination, a hill above a bend in the river. A path led to the top, where I could see the leaf-thatched roof of a hut. Camilo said, "The man who lives here is named Noma. He's a brother of Nenke the shaman and he's a shaman too." When we landed, a man, a woman, and two boys around ten delightedly descended the path to meet us. The man and woman were each wearing a pair of dirty gray underwear, the boys no clothes at all. There was some discussion in Waorani and they all shook my hand. The man and woman did so very gently, a soft touch of the palms that seemed to say, "Let's be tame with each other." The bigger boy gripped my hand firmly like someone checking the muscles of the neck of a boa. The smaller boy gripped softly, shocking me when I felt a vestigial sixth finger dangling from the first knuckle of his pinky. He had another on the other hand. Each of his broad feet had six functional toes.

Pata swung my pack ashore. Obe and Camilo shook hands with me firmly. Camilo yanked the cord on the thirty-horsepower Yamaha outboard motor. The thing coughed and sputtered to life. A bit more discussion in Wao, and the canoe swung around and roared back upriver.

***

Pata speaks some Spanish. Noma speaks very little of it, his wife and sons none. We're on a hill overlooking a bend in the river. The house is dirt-floored, shaped like an equilateral triangle when seen from either end, 15 feet high at the peak of the roof. The roof, made of leaves, leaked in the rain that poured down last night. The triangular end walls, made of vertical slats, let in air and light. Leaning against a wall is a blowgun and a cluster of half a dozen all-but-black, three-meter-long, seven-centimeter-wide, jagged-tipped spears.

The spears are worth lingering on for a moment. They're made of chonta, the previously-mentioned hardest wood in the forest. The bottom end is pointed, and fairly sharp, so the implement can be stored upright, stuck in the ground. The forward tip of each spear is jagged in two sections. The first, at the end, is a row of teeth that guides the implement deeper into its target and makes it hard to pull out. The second section, closer to the haft, is an identical row of teeth pointing in the opposite direction, making the spear harder to parry with a hand or arm.

Along with the four people, two birds live in the hut. One is a parrot and the other an immature gray bird

133

with a wide beak—a *potu*, Pata says. Outside, on a horizontal pole under a little roof, lives a spider monkey, a watch-animal, subsisting on plantains, fellating himself, and alerting the humans if anything comes near.

Noma is fiftyish and handsome, standoffish, with sharp shaman-eyes and big stretched-out rubber band earlobes.

His wife, much younger than he is, is friendly, and pretty, too, though her front teeth are missing and her breasts droop. Her body is pantherish in power and weathered by hard work.

The older son, Kowane, struts around, joking loudly, making his parents laugh, stalking his little brother and attempting to strike. He's the spitting image of his father.

The younger son, Tunae, the one with extra digits, doesn't always feel like getting chased, but puts up with it. He's shy and dreamy and looks like their mom.

As I write, sitting in this palm fiber hammock, the two boys are resting their chins on my knees. Two heads loll, looking at me through wondering brown windows. Trying to glimpse the world outside the forest through the lens of this stranger.

Now they've been poking and tugging the hair on my legs and chest. Studying. Gathering data. Wao adults have nearly no body hair.

They talk with Pata. He tells me they say I look like a woolly monkey.

Now the three of them are leafing through my copy of *Finnegans Wake*.

This morning, the four of us went hunting with blowguns. Pata killed a toucan. I took a shot at a dove but, of course, missed.

Plucked, gutted, scrawny, Mister Toucan took a hot bath with some yuca—that long, smooth, white, somewhat-potatoish root vegetable I'd enjoyed with the Secoyas—and ended up tasting pretty good, though he was a tough old bird.

Over the last few days, we've also eaten boiled yellow plantains; *paujil,* a little black wild turkey that sings like a flute in the forest at dawn; and woolly monkey (like a little human corpse with a tail, covered in burnt fur; the brain is like gray guacamole; the liver is not bad).

Only thing I have left from the market in Coca is three-quarters of a jar of Nescafé.

***

Need to practice with the blowgun.

***

Kowane's sense of humor: he farts and blows it at his brother or me with the paujil-feather fan they use for getting the fire going.

The boys' mom is making a beverage Pata calls *chicha.* Each day, she produces enough for the next day, for her, her husband, her sons, Pata, and me.

She boils yuca, mashes it, chews a mouthful of it, grins at me with it pushing like a pale tongue through the broad gap in her teeth, spits it in the pot, chews, spits, chews, spits, then covers it with the lid and leaves it to ferment overnight.

Each day, she digs into the previous day's batch (she owns two dented aluminum pots), mixes the mash with fresh water in a gourd, and serves it.

It's sour, nourishing, mildly alcoholic. And, whenever I manage to forget I'm drinking spit (which is not often), it's delicious.

135

Now she sings a simple, repetitive, insistent, nasal melody while weaving a vine-basket.

***

Tunae has a bunch of open sores on his head, so I got out my disinfectant cream and asked Pata to extend my offer to put it on him. Agreed to and done. Then there was some discussion in this language like rubber bands being strummed. The mom came over and pulled her gray underwear straight down off her left ass cheek, exposing another open sore.

I thought, *Her husband! His spears!*

Carefully, carefully applied I the cream to the pustulating wound.

While Pata foraged for firewood, the family and I bathed, all of us naked, in a stream behind the house. The adults wanted me to be naked with them, I thought, so we'd know each other better. And so they could study me.

In the evening, Noma made curare, poison for his blowgun darts. Resinous liquid dripped from the tip of a wrapped leaf. He applied the finished poison to about 30 darts and stacked them by the fire so they formed a little drying rack.

Me, I'm drying knowledge onto the darts of literature, getting them ready to poison ignorance.

***

"Pata," I said, "I want to be by myself for a while in the forest to pray and mediate. Would you please ask Noma if that's all right?"

Pata nodded, talked with the shaman for a while, came back shaking his head. "He says the jaguars would eat you."

"No," I said, remembering the jaguar dream I'd had at fifteen. "They wouldn't hurt me." Those jaguars had needed my help.

"You're a friend of the jaguars, eh?" Pata cracked a smile.

"Yes," I said, determined to push the issue. I was sure I'd be safe. I was the protagonist of the story. And I was afraid of falling behind on my spiritual quest. It would be more dangerous *not* to meet the jaguars. "Isn't there someplace I could go around here? I spent four days on a hilltop in Mexico. I want to do something like that here."

"Noma says there's an old hut, but it's falling down, and the jaguars would walk in and eat you."

"Just give me a spear," I said, exasperated. "I'll be fine."

Pata spoke to Noma again. The older man laughed and replied. Pata turned back to me. "No. He says it would make too much trouble for him if you got killed."

"OK," I conceded. I wouldn't go against the shaman's wishes.

***

Commotion in the hut: Noma's wife spotted a rustling in the treetops on the other side of the river: monkeys! We raced down to the family canoe and sped to the opposite bank! Pata's muzzle-loader boomed and a black body plummeted through vegetation. As the troop of monkeys scattered, Noma tagged another with a blowgun dart. It didn't die, but the curare slowed it, and he and Pata dashed headlong through the jungle, following its faint rustling in the canopy. The rest of us trailed them. Crossing a stream on a log, I slipped and fell in water up to my neck. I clambered out, poured the water out of my too-small rubber boots, and pressed on, reminding myself

137

again of Watthorímetro Thermofascio, the space alien who wanted to be a rabbi.

Noma and Pata took turns shooting the shaman's blowgun. Sometimes the monkey would pause in a tree and they'd shout at it to move on. Once Noma grabbed a heavy vine that hung from the canopy of a tree that the monkey had paused in, and he slammed the vine again and again against the trunk, bellowing up at the terrified animal. Pata told me if it died in the crotch of a tree, he or Noma would have to climb up to get it.

A few hundred meters later, the paralysis increased and the monkey became confined to one limb of one tree. They took shot after shot at it as it moved back and forth, crying, pleading with them to spare its life, just that once. They laughed.

Pata took a dart and, as he'd done each time, inscribed a notch around the shaft just below the poisoned tip with a piranha jaw that dangled by a palm fiber string from the bamboo dart quiver. The cut was to make the dart tip more likely to break off inside the animal. Then he took a pinch of cottony fluff from inside a gourd and wrapped the fluff around the other end of the dart, five centimeters from the end. He loaded the dart in the mouthpiece of the blowgun and handed it to me. The weapon was made of dense, dark chonta palm wood, surprisingly heavy. I took a deep breath and blew. I caught a glimpse of the dart rising, not high, then veering away and getting lost in the foliage. Noma and Pata laughed. "Not bad," Pata said kindly. "You just need to practice."

He took the blowgun back and blasted two more darts up at the animal. It lost its balance and plummeted. He ran down and fished it out of a stream. It was still alive when he cut a vine and tied the end of its tail to its neck and handed it to me to carry over my shoulder like a wet, furry sports bag with a strap. We set off for home. The monkey died on my back. As I slogged on in wet socks and cramped boots, I was glad I could be useful in at least this way. Back at the hut, Noma's wife—her name's Ayamo, I learned—put the corpse in the fire to char most of the fur off, then sliced open the abdomen, discarded inedible organs I couldn't identify, chopped off the head, limbs and tail, put the body, limbs, head and edible organs into an aluminum pot with yuca and water, and hung it over the fire, where it's boiling now.

***

We had monkey for dinner last night. There's plenty left over, stewing in the blackened aluminum cauldron over the low, crackling fire. This rainy morning, Noma and Ayamo went out on some errand. The entertainment for Pata and me was watching the boys chase each other all around the house, up into the rafters, and out into the rain, throwing spears of long grass at each other, having a ball learning to kill.

Kowane's watching me write, sitting beside me, holding my left knee.

This morning, Pata asked me, "Europe—what do they do?" When I hesitated, he prodded, "They work airplanes?" (*¿Trabajan aviones?*) I figured he either wanted to know if they work *with* airplanes or if they make them. I answered yes, they do. He nodded, partially satisfied, filing the imperfect information away. I had a question for him, too: "Does Noma have ayahuasca?" He went to talk with Noma. I wanted to get back into that ayahuasca headspace as soon as possible, and this would be an amazing place to do it. After a long discussion, though, Pata came back with a short answer: "No." Shit.

He and I talked about ayahuasca. He's never tried it and doesn't want to. He knows a bit about it, though, or

139

thinks he does, anyway. "When you drink ayahuasca, the Devil will come," he informed me.

"But I don't want the Devil to come."

"Too bad!" Pata cracked a smile. "He'll come anyway."

Last night I couldn't get comfortable, waking up several times with various parts of my body numb or just cold. I got ready to sleep on a sheet of plastic on the bumpy dirt floor. My chinos and t-shirt were damp from the fall in the stream, so I lay on the sarape, wearing my swimsuit, my plaid cotton shirt, my plastic rain pants, and my silk undershirt wrapped around my feet. My rain jacket served as a pillow.

The sleeping positions of all of us are as follows: Noma, Ayamo and one boy (last night, Tunae) on a small wooden platform between two fires; Pata and the other boy (last night, Kowane) in the hammock, perpendicular to the platform and next to one of the fires; and I, parallel to the platform, on the other side of a fire, perpendicular to the hammock. Last night Tunae was using a dirty shirt of Noma's as a pillow, but other than that, nobody has used any extra clothes, blankets, or anything like them to sleep. Body heat helps, and keeping the fires going all night.

In a dream, I'm in the front hall of the house where I grew up. My stepdad Walt warns me there might be an intruder in the attic. I grab a baseball bat and sprint up the two flights of stairs. At the top I find two Walts, or maybe Walt and a twin brother. They stare at me suspiciously, and one asks me, "What do you think you're doing with that bat?" I suddenly wonder who the Walt downstairs is.

When I woke up, I reflected that there was no trace of my mom in the dream. That worries me, since she shows up in my dreams a lot. Maybe she's dead. Ever since news of her brother's death came to her over the

140

psychic telegraph wire, I've been in the habit of searching my dreams for clues that somebody has died.

I lay in the dark, listening to the Waorani breathing in their sleep, and I remembered that both my parents came close to dying in the past year—breast cancer, heart attack—and were saved by medical technology. They would have died if they'd been Waorani, Secoya, or Cora.

And how will I feel when they really die, one and then the other? I'll deal with it. It's the kind of thing you can only deal with. *Aguántalo,* don Joaquín said. It hurts, and hurts, and hurts, and little by little you feel a little better. When I was a kid I used to wake up crying, imagining that one or the other of them had died, imagining how I'll feel when it does happen; imagining going to the shore of a deserted lake and yelling and screaming and trying to be heard by them, and not getting any answer. I still feel sheltered by them. When I went outside at dawn, wondering if my mom's breast cancer had recurred, I thought, *Maybe I have a few good years in store before tragedy strikes again.* I paid some dues when I was younger. I spent some time in Hell.

"Nanda! Nanda!" my hosts shout. I go look. Some kind of big water mammal, maybe capybara, maybe otter, cruising down the river in front of the house.

It's curious that now that Walt's gone, my mom and dad are suddenly so sweet on each other. My dad's always been sweet on my mom, but now she's gotten to the point of reminiscing fondly about their honeymoon. For nine months between 1966 and 1967, they wandered like Adam and Eve from Baltimore to Israel, Turkey, Greece, Italy, France, England, and Ireland. When they flew back to the States, she was pregnant with me.

My mom even told me recently how she became interested in my dad: she saw a life-sized charcoal drawing he'd made of a crouching female nude. He'd drawn it with

141

a single line without taking the charcoal off the paper. Someone who could do that must be pretty remarkable, she thought. I believe I owe my existence to that drawing.

Chiaroscuro. In keeping my eyes out for a wife, for many years, I've been looking for someone who wouldn't do to me what my mom did to my dad. At the same time, I've been semiconsciously enacting psychodramas with my girlfriends that replicate what I think happened between the two of them. With Jennifer, for instance. Soon after she and I got together, I lost interest in her personality, and when she broke up with me, I was crushed and wanted her back. At least with Lily, I don't feel like I'm playing that particular game.

I'd like to stay in Latin America until I figure out my life. Maybe Lily can join me here. I'm sick of walking around harming myself and others. Here, as in Mexico, I don't feel like I'm on a treadmill. My mind doesn't endlessly loop crazy thoughts. The forest is strong enough to break through all that. Or I'm strong enough here to do it myself—a large mammal roaring defiance of all that has ever sullied his soul.

Pata's watching me write while he fans the flames under the cooking fire with the black paujil-feather fan.

Now he reclines in the hammock to open and close the many blades of the Victorinox Swiss Army knife that the last visitor gave Noma.

Earlier, I asked about the visitor.

"She was a scientist," Pata said. "From Chinamarca."

"Dinamarca [Denmark]?" I said.

"No, *China*marca."

"China?"

"No, China*marca*."

"There's no country called Chinamarca."

"There is," he corrected me. "That's where she was from. She wanted to take me there for a visit, but my wife wouldn't let me go."

"OK." No sense in arguing. I'm apparently in an alternate reality where there's a country called Chinamarca. Chinamark. I wonder what the population looks like—blond with epicanthic folds?—and how their society is organized, what their literature discusses, what their traditional dances and clothing represent, what animals they hunt.

That brings me to this other dream from last night. Holy crap. I go into a hut where Noma lives. He's sitting on a hammock, chatting with Pata, who's standing. Noma has a gaping hole in his abdomen, wide open, up to the ribcage, like the monkeys when Ayamo butchered them. Guts dangle in the cave of his belly. He jokes with Pata and they share a laugh.

The scene changes and we're all in a cavern. Living viscera the size of men hang from the stone ceiling.

As I woke up, I remembered inlakesh, the Mexican idea Alberto told Franco and me about, "I'm another you."

He
was
what he killed
&
what he killed
was
he.

On the sixth morning it was time to start heading back. Pata and I said goodbye to the shaman and his family and set out for Pata's village, an eight-hour hike away. I was wearing the size 43 rubber boots. Every step

143

impacted my toes. The path led up and down low hills. The rain started and stopped and started again. After two hours Pata offered to exchange packs with me. The Wao was much smaller than I, but much stronger, and he cheerfully shouldered the heavier burden. After two more hours he remarked that we were going too slowly to make the trip in eight hours. Then he suggested another rest. I lay flat on my back, panting for air, then yanked off my boots and massaged my toes. Pata, alert, curious, politely posed a question that had apparently been on his mind for a while. "The world," he said, "what shape is it?"

Before starting to answer, I held still, letting the question wash over me, watching the trees that surged up (or down, depending on one's perspective) to the sky. I'd read in the Explorers Club that the Waorani traditionally believed the world was flat, and I gathered Pata had heard that outsiders had a different idea. Coincidentally, I'd recently been thinking that if one figured in the fourth dimension, time, the world would look something like a complicated, elongated corkscrew as it spun through revolutions around a sun that revolved around the center of a galaxy that moved through the universe away from where the Big Bang happened. But I couldn't explain that in Spanish.

Thinking back to Cola's question, I remembered from my college class in astronomy that no one really understands how gravity works. I began tentatively, "We used to think the world was flat, like you-all do. Now we think it's round, like a ball. Maybe in the future we'll see it differently. But it seems to be like a giant ball, and it's so big that it looks flat from where we stand on it, but when you go up very high you can see that it's round. And somehow, everything sticks to it. No one knows exactly why, but when something is very, very big, it pulls on other things." Pata nodded, somewhat satisfied with this

144

explanation, maybe because it echoed what he'd heard from the scientist from Chinamark.

We set out again. Soon the path vanished. A while after that, Pata remarked, without slowing down, "We're lost."

As I stumbled on, and the earth caroomed through space on its attenuated corkscrew path, I numbed my body and withdrew into my mind. Memories rose and fell. The rain came and went. Every step I took, my toes jammed into the tips of the boots. I was afraid I might lose the nails of my big toes. I moved ahead robotically, pondering my unhappy relationship to my parents. *I'm a fuck-up. I lean on them. They give financial support to their fragile, emotionally damaged only child in hopes that he may one day become well. For my part, in relying on them, it's like I'm suing them for the mess they made of my early childhood. When will I get beyond this and stand on my own? I need them to help me, which convinces me that I'm weak, so I need them to help me again.*

Back to the jungle. I remembered the Waorani boys, Kowane and Tunae, gently leading me by the hand from place to place as if I were a large wild animal needing domestication.

I remembered their grandfather Noma, a shaman without ayahuasca, who never looked at me directly except when handing me a monkey limb from the pot while beaming a huge grin—this magician who survived by consuming his karmic doppelgangers in the forest.

I remembered what Carlos had said about eating monkey, and I wished it would make me even a little stronger.

I remembered the time I stood up too quickly in Noma's hut and got a head rush, my first since the one on the hilltop in Mexico. When I got a head rush in the United States, I'd feel an overwhelming self-consciousness, a certainty that others were thinking unflattering thoughts

145

about me, their negative impressions confirmed by the fact that I was standing there swaying with a spaced-out expression on my face. I was too embarrassed to ask anyone about this and thus never learned if it was pure paranoia or not. With the Waoranis, though, I felt an equally strong sense of comfort. No movement into the spirit world, as had happened above El Nopal, but a feeling that everything was happening just as it needed to. Specifically, it didn't seem odd that I was visiting these people. It seemed the most normal thing in the world.

My feet aching, I kept trudging behind Pata. I remembered Ayamo. Her missing front teeth. The open sore on her ass that I smeared with disinfectant gel but should have scraped out and washed first. The imprint, when she turned over, of the weave of the palm-fiber hammock on the skin of her breasts. And the time she and I were alone in the hut and she looked at me as if inviting me to make love to her. This made me imagine vectors of HIV transmission through the hookers of Coca, and then (and not for the first time) what it would be like to be body-pierced by her husband's barbed spears—maybe just one of them, or maybe many of them until I looked like Labaka after the Tagaeri had had their way with him. Then I thought I didn't want to risk fathering a child that would grow up a stranger to me. And finally, I didn't want to be unfaithful to Lily—which struck me as curious, now, as I trudged through the forest banging my toes into my boots. It's a strange sort of morality that lets me have an affair with a married woman but won't let me cheat on her. In sum, in the moment the offer was made, I froze, and Ayamo turned back to the basket she was weaving.

When Pata got back from hunting that day, he and I were talking, and I said something to him about Noma being Ayamo's husband. Pata said, "No, he's not her husband, he's her father-in-law. It's just that his wife died

146

and her husband drowned when his canoe turned over, so the two of them live together now and raise the boys." So maybe on that level it would have been fine to make love to her.

As I trudged behind Pata, walking on my heels and the sides of my feet to try to protect my toes, I thought how strange it was that people would live their whole lives along rivers but be unable to swim. I supposed it was just a development that had never happened in their culture. A valuable skill to have.

Death by drowning, by sickness, by spear. I wondered again how death would feel when it happened to me. When I was little, my mom said it was like a candle being blown out. One moment there's life and light, the next moment nothing at all. *Late one summer night in '74, I'm six, in the way-back of the family's four-door reddish-brown 1971 Chevrolet Nomad, which is surging down a highway in New Mexico. Street lights fling white spider webs across the ceiling of the car. My two older stepbrothers and my older stepsister ride silently in the middle seat. My mom and Walter are in front, one driving, the other navigating with the Rand McNally atlas, trying to find a campground. I think of that candle going out, the fear overwhelms me, and I burst into tears, screaming, "I don't wanna die! I don't wanna die!" as the three young teens in the middle seat drowsily try to ignore me.*

I followed Pata onto another fallen log across another stream. *That must be why I write—so my thoughts can live on after me.* There was mud on the log. Pata stopped and said, "Look. ¡Tigre!" He indicated a jaguar footprint in the mud. It must've been fresh: rain had been falling half an hour before. I stared at the deep, clear print for a second. Where was the cat now? As I crossed the fallen log, the Nomad became a giant jaguar on whose back I clung. Then a black and yellow helicopter I was piloting over a

147

forest of giant flowers. What had Labaka felt when he went out to die?

There'd been a weird episode on day three of my visit when the family heard the sound of an oil company helicopter. They and Pata got really excited and ran outside the hut and, until it disappeared, jumped up and down and screamed and waved at it. Even dignified Noma. I was ashamed of them. They were acting like children.

Now, though, I figured they must've been thinking there was a chance the copter might drop down something good to them.

I thought about something else I didn't write down when it happened. Once I was standing and talking with Pata when Kowane suddenly sprang forward and grabbed my crotch, then sprang back, laughing. I was shocked. What the fuck? That couldn't have just happened. Boys don't pounce on men's dicks like cats on mice.

He did it again the next day. I yelled, "No!!!" This was short for, "Don't do that to non-Waorani! It freaks us out!" By that time, I'd realized it was a game. He played it with his brother and with Pata. A sport, a martial art, a bonding ritual. They scored points on each other.

Ever since Adam and Eve, we Westerners have covered our dicks and limited the contact other people have to them. For Waorani, though, dicks are *public* parts.

I wasn't prepared to be part of this game. In my haste to convince the kid that his actions were wrong in my culture, I broke a rule of his culture: I was loud, nasty, a spoilsport. What a jerk.

Stop foot! A loop of vine brought me out of my head. I disentangled and walked on.

I passed a cluster of red and yellow flowers growing on the trunk of a tree as if they'd leapt up from the ground and clung there. They brought me back to the flower

148

gardens my mom used to plant in the springtime in front of the house. At the edge of the dirt, where it met the sidewalk, she had a row of round, gray fieldstones, half-buried; behind them she'd plant a row of marigolds, lion-headed soldiers, to keep out the bugs; then snapdragons, snarling, yellow and pink and blue maws agape; then the rest of the jostling, brilliant throng. At the back, near the bushes, tall, spindly, bifurcating stalks like long green sparks presented purple blooms with yellow centers to the sun. My mom said these were "cosmos." I knew things often got their names from what they looked like. Someone must have figured these were shaped like the universe.

The garden's perennials grew by themselves, but the annuals had to be bought, half-grown, from a nursery in a huge greenhouse fragrant with blossoms and damp dirt. Another vine caught my boot and I skidded to a stop, unhooked myself, and was back in the memory, a young boy staring at a table laden with pansies. Their purples and yellows were so intense as to blot out the universe, until my mom called me to follow her to the counter, where she took the blue Pilot ballpoint pen from the right front pocket of her brown corduroys—at my eye level—and wrote out a check from her leather purse. Then we carried the plastic flats of swaying, half-grown flowers outside to the Chevy Nomad, our car, our jaguar, our copter, our migratory living room of steel origami, glass, rubber, and chrome.

And always, again, the pounding of toes into rubber boots.

A snatch of more recent dialog echoed: my mom saying, "You're running away from something," and me countering, "No, I'm running toward something." I imagined speaking reasonably to her: "The mythological way of seeing things and the scientific way of seeing things

149

are both valid. They're like our two eyes. Neither one of them sees everything, but they can work together and give us depth perception—a better view than we would have with only one of them." This was a concession. A compromise. But she didn't buy it. In my head, her voice responded with no specific content, just the tone, dismissing what I'd said. It felt like a stab in the chest. I lost my patience and raged at her. "You don't want me to take drugs. Would you rather I was a *chainsmoker* like your dad? Would you rather I was a *drunk* like your brother? You taught me to think independently. You taught me to follow an idea to its logical conclusion, exploring it every step of the way. And now that I'm doing that, you don't like the results! Even though it was *your methods* that brought me here! I used the intelligence that *you developed* to form my vision of the world, and now you want to stomp out that vision like so much burning paper! I won't let you! NO!" I felt myself punching her in the mouth with all my strength.

I halted, swaying, holding onto the mossy trunk of a tree, anger melting into remorse. *Breathe,* I reminded myself.

"Pata," I called, "I need a break."

He stopped and opened a plastic bag and we rested and snacked on soft bland yuca chunks that Ayamo had boiled for us.

When we were walking again, a softcover book bobbed up amid the wet trunks of the trees. My mom or stepdad had left it on a low shelf. At six I was an early and curious reader. Alone, I opened the book. It contained black and white photos from the Vietnam War. A suspected Viet Cong faced the camera with his hands tied behind his back and blood streaming from his smashed nose and mouth. Another photo showed a Viet Cong executed by being dragged by his feet behind a halftrack

150

down a road in the jungle. I knew from what the grownups said that my country was to blame for the torture, and I was ashamed.

Now, years later, I was in a different jungle hurrying to keep up with a man who looked like a sturdy Vietnamese as he tried to find the way to his home village. The thought that we weren't in a war zone made me suddenly happy. Another red and yellow flowering epiphyte on a tree trunk reminded me of my mom's garden again. I wished I could show it to her. I imagined saying to her, "Ma, I've recently had an experience that has changed me forever, a ceremony that has put me in touch with the hidden springs of life. I love my life again and I have a purpose. I'm very happy and I want to share that with you." And this time she didn't say anything, but nodded and smiled, pleased for me.

A fantasy.

At dusk, Pata called a halt. He wielded his machete and built a lean-to shelter, then kindled a fire with the help of some diesel from a plastic bottle. After sharing with me more of Ayamo's yuca, he plucked a bunch of big stiff leaves and drove their stems into the ground one by one so they stayed upright and delineated a low barrier around the lean-to. I said, "What is this?"

Pata said, "With the fire and the leaves, the jaguars won't attack us."

Really? I thought, nodding. I lay on my belly with my arms over my head and closed my eyes. My arms become two forest paths that diverge before me. I head off down the right one.

Accompanying a shifty, forty-something, white salesman, I enter a cottage in the woods where an elderly African-American couple live. My companion plans to cheat them out of their scanty possessions. We all sit down at a table. The swindler begins his evil work, offering a

151

small mirror in exchange for a huge, freshly caught fish. The old black man just gives him the fish, saying, "Keep your mirror, I already have one," indicating a large mirror on the wall with an ornate frame. The swindler offers a plastic rat-tail comb for the wall mirror and the old man stuns him by taking it off the wall and giving it to him.

The old woman says, "For the last few months, he's had the power to fish for whatever he's wanted. He goes down to any body of water, be it ocean or puddle, wishes for something, throws in his line and pulls out whatever it is. We're not sure if the power is in him or in the fishing pole, but either way, we don't feel right taking someone else's stuff in exchange for things that are given so freely to us." She shows the swindler and me two photos, from their recent vacation in California, of her husband effortlessly pulling from the waves a Cadillac and a killer whale.

The scene changes and I'm in a house with my dad and my dad's dad. I have some of the spiritual power that the old black man had. There's a dead white man on the floor. I take a buck knife and cut off his right hand. I transfer the knife to my left hand and painlessly cut off my own right hand. I put down the knife and affix the corpse's hand to my stump, just to prove I can. My new hand works perfectly. It's a bit smaller than my old one. There's a scar around the wrist. I'm proud of myself, and I walk around flexing my new right hand, holding my old right hand in my left.

Then I notice again the discrepancy in the sizes of my hands. I realize the operation is permanent. I'll always have a dead man's hand in place of my own perfectly good one—which, at this moment, starts digging its nails into my left palm, asking to be put back on its wrist. It's still alive, and it's as warm as it ever was, and it feels exactly the same to my left hand, but I can't feel what it feels. And it has its own unfamiliar weight and personality.

I take my three hands to my father's father for help. I can see only the top half of his mostly-bald head, with its wisps of gray hair around the sides and its liver-colored spots. He exclaims, "Noma! He makes gold hands." He means that the shaman is behind what happened, and this is a technique that Noma uses, an activity he performs.

Only the top of his head visible, my grandfather outlines two possible scenarios. In one, Noma performed the hand transplant and deluded me into thinking I'd done it myself. In the other scenario, the operation never occurred at all: it's just something Noma made me believe, and the hand that looks like a corpse's hand is actually my own, on my wrist, right where it belongs.

I woke in the gray dawn with my hands back to normal and the sounds of the forest pouring into my head. Without moving, I replayed and analyzed my dreams. The old couple represented the forest, able to produce anything, giving it away for free. In the second part of the dream, I had some of that nature magic, but I abused it. Or maybe Noma had only tricked me into thinking I had. Was it an initiation? A crime? Many interpretations existed in parallel at different levels. I ruminated, like a howler monkey on a mouthful of leaves, thinking, *Everything has an infinite number of explanations anyway, just as everything happens for an infinite number of reasons.*

Over a breakfast of the last of the boiled yuca from the plastic bag, I told Pata my dream. He listened and nodded, then replied with a dream of his own in which he rode across an ocean on the back of a turtle and ate soup with a white woman.

We finished off the boiled yuca and licked our fingers. On my abused feet I put a pair of dry socks and the rubber boots, and we slogged off toward his village. I

153

thought, *Noma put the hand of the dead on me. Shamanism's the hand of the dead. People on this path are alive and dead at the same time. That's what gives knowledge of the next world. Like old one-eyed Odin with his empty eye-cave staring into the void.*

***

Before midday, Pata and I reached his village and were celebrated by dogs and kids. The trip he'd thought would take eight hours had taken twelve. He hadn't imagined anyone would move as slowly through the forest as I did.

We stayed in the little village of ten or fifteen souls for a couple of days. We ate fresh and smoked armadillo, and plenty of boiled yuca, and *naranjillas,* sour-sweet orange fruits that grew on bushes. I slept on the dirt floor of Pata's hut, incompletely wrapped in my sarape, on top of the skin of a jaguar. The nails of my big toes turned stormy and purple-black.

Then I wanted to be alone in nature again, and the people let me move into a deserted house on the riverbank so I could fast from food and water as I had in Mexico. They were pretty sure no jaguar would come around here. We agreed I'd stay five days, then be picked up by canoe.

The palm frond roof of the hut was falling down, but one section still provided a body's worth of shelter from the rain.

Surrounded by the buzzing, squawking forest, I sculpted a face out of clay and stuck it to a house post. I hungered and thirsted, swam, and sang King Crimson songs from the tape the Waorani had socialized. I wondered if the cheese I had bought was still on top of Señora Sabas's refrigerator. I hoped Ray had made it back

154

to Ohio safely. I prayed for my family and friends and for everyone I had met on my journeys.

At dusk, wandering upriver, I found the mud cuneiformed with the tracks of the web-footed capybara, largest rodent in the world. I thought that if I had been a Dogon shaman, I might have been able to read the future there.

Over the next days, I wrote love letters to Lily. I wrote a long list of foods I wanted us to eat together: cheese blintzes with sour cream and applesauce, sauteed-onion-green-pepper-tomato-and-cheese omelets, Korean-style spicy fish and rice with kimchi, pancakes with embedded chunks of fresh plums, deep fried vanilla ice cream....

I read aloud the four-dimensional voices of *Finnegans Wake*—which, like the voice in my peyote vision, combined languages and devised neologisms. Neologisms devised and languages combined: vision, peyote, my in-voice, the like which wake Finnegans of voices' dimension—all for thee, a loud red eye.

Didn't have any spiritual experiences. But was happy to be by myself. Days with nobody to talk to. Just wave at Waorani paddling near to make sure I'm OK. Happy to hang out in the shallows of the riverbank, soaking in the sun and thinking how amphibians must feel.

Kept hoping Pata's brother Miguel would come and pick me up with his speedboat, as we'd sort of arranged.

Scooped up another handful of mud and sculpted a second human face on the second post of the hut.

When the five days were over, the good Pata came to pick me up in a canoe. As he steadied the craft so I could step in, he said, "Last night I dreamt my brother came down to pick you up. That means he'll be here tomorrow."

Well, all right then.

Next day, in fact, Miguel buzzed down the river in his silver speedboat, spent an hour visiting, and zoomed me back upriver to the village at the former oil camp where the road began.

I remembered what Jeremy Carver had said about Waoranis checking him out through his dreams. *There must be something to the Waorani dream thing. Can you learn that like a foreign language? How long would I have to stay around here before I could do it myself?*

***

Back in Coca, among hookers and oilmen, I experienced a strong intestinal upset. At the Hotel Auca, it kept me on the toilet half the night. Though I'd purified all the water I'd drunk, some microbes had gotten to me, probably from the half-cooked monkeys. Biting the microbes to death didn't work. They just colonized my meat planet and started breeding. I guessed the reason I didn't have any spiritual experiences on my fast is that millions of microbes were making mad love in my sacral chakra. The vibration's all wrong for spiritual work.

In the morning, black ladies in bright dresses and head-cloths were vending food under parasols at the Coca market. They said, "Hey, come have some breakfast."

I said, "Do you know anything good for intestinal problems?"

A lady said, "Sure thing. This dish here is called *guatita*. Cow intestines, boiled until tender, in peanut sauce on top of rice. Absolute best thing for gut problems. It's got all the vitamins your gut needs." Her friends confirmed this and I sat down.

The rice and peanut and oil made the guatita (*wa-TI-ta*) delicious; the unfamiliar texture of the intestine proved as soothing as it was disgusting. A cold, sweet, orange Fanta washed it down.

My gut calmed somewhat, though I still felt weak and trembly. I made it back to Quito by bus. Eager to get to know the city, I watched an avant-garde theater production called Octopus's Garden—named after the Beatles song—and got stoned multiple times with a deaf guy I'd met at a co-ed public bath.

Then I flew up to Mexico City and took a bus to Guadalajara, where the nails of my big toes finally fell off.

11. The Fox

Savoring a beef tamal in my friends' kitchen, rubbing the belly of their little white dog Towi with the side of my bare foot (keeping my nailless big toe away), I gazed at a crack in the paint on the wall that I remembered from the last time I'd sat there. It was like a canyon on Mars seen from high above, or a fissure in the solidity of reality itself. I reflected that my visit to the Waoranis had pushed me past where I'd been comfortable going. Killing the baby monkey, eating other monkeys' charred limbs and boiled livers and brains, the Tagaeri hooting in the forest, the jaguar kid pouncing on my dick, the hike that knocked the nails off my toes, the population explosion in my guts—the cumulative effect of these things disturbed me more than I'd expected to be disturbed.

Still. I thought back to the conversation I'd had two years earlier at Kosher Co-op with Jeremy Carver. I wished I could let him know that overall, my journey to the southern lands had been a great success. In the eight months since leaving the States, I'd become fluent in Spanish. I'd stayed with indigenous people and been part of their worlds. I'd met spirits in the desert, and in the ceremony of yagé, I'd felt astounding joy, and been welcomed into the tradition—even the dogs had agreed. I murmured Nezahualcoyotl's prayer: *Thank you. I want more.*

My hosts put me in their sky-blue VW Beetle and whisked me through the dust-brown city of Guadalajara to a free clinic to deal with my intestinal problem. The microscope slide of my fecal sample created a sensation. The staff crowded round to peer at the exotic rainforest parasites like visitors to a zoo.

I decided to make one last try to visit the Huichols before heading into Texas, where I would meet my dad, who was visiting the editors of his art appreciation textbook. The main Huichol town was called San Andrés Cohamiata. I headed out of Guadalajara on a bus. Swallowing the pills the doctors gave me to poison my intruders, I read the last confusing page of *Finnegans Wake*—including the beginning of the sentence that ended on the first page. Later that day, as the medicine was taking effect, I was given chips of dried peyote—like peyote jerky—by an Argentinian hippie, and I feel millions of tiny creatures screaming as they die in my gut. Trying to memorize a few words in Thai to say to Lily, I murmur over the micro-screams, *Phm rak khun!*, I love you!

The bus routes ended and I started hitchhiking. One morning in a small town at the local office of the National Indigenous Institute, I met three Huichols in their seventies who were on pilgrimage. They were sharply dressed in white clothes with multicolored embroidery and wore feathered straw hats whose brims dangled bright beaded pendants. The oldest man was nearly blind with cataracts, but two bright pink flowers were tucked under his hatband, pointing forward like headlights. He told me he and his friends were heading away from San Andrés Cohamiata. Not hitchhiking, he specified, but walking. He showed me a colorful, embroidered pouch of peyote. "We take one or two of these in the morning and we can walk all day without needing to eat or drink," he said.

"What about the visions? What do you see?"

"Sometimes the shadows under a tree look like writhing snakes," he said. "Or the sun says to you, 'Sit down, listen, I have something to say to you.'"

"Can I buy a peyote from you?"

Without a word, the old man takes the largest peyote from his pouch and hands it to me. I hand him all the coins in my pocket, two or three dollars' worth, and we part, wishing each other well.

159

A couple of managers from the Coca-Cola company agree to bring me toward San Andrés. Standing in the back of their pickup truck, I surf the dry, sun-flooded, waving, craggy hills, which are thronged with cactuses and dotted with dark blue *urraca* birds, bigger cousins of the North American Blue Jay, with black crests, white breasts, and long dark blue tail feathers.

The Coke guys dropped me at a point on the highway where a road led off toward my destination. As the sun was setting, I headed down the rocky road into a fragrant forest of pine. Like a slumbering yellow mastodon, a bulldozer rested at the side of the road. A fourteen-foot cargo truck and a pickup were parked nearby. A campfire was burning. Six guys were sitting around it. I called out, *"Buenas noches."*

The men welcomed me, wanted news of my travels, and invited me to sleep by their fire. They were a work crew. Their job was to use the bulldozer to scrape the road leading to San Andrés Cohamiata.

"We've been out here six days," one of them said. "On the first day of work, the bulldozer broke down. The part we need is back in the city of Tepic, two days' drive away. So our colleague drove away in search of the part. And we have nothing to do but to try to kill the fox."

"The fox?" I asked.

"He ate our chorizo the first night we were out here. And every night since then, he's come back trying to steal stuff. Look up above the bulldozer. Hanging from a tree branch. Can you see what it is?"

"Is it a plastic bag full of chorizo?"

"It is, precisely, a plastic bag full of chorizo. The fox can't reach it there, but its smell may bring him so we can kill him."

"Ah." I hoped they wouldn't kill the fox.

160

Night landed on the earth like a starry bat. Fragrant pine logs crackled in the fire. Sparks leapt up and smoke sought the Milky Way. One of the men reminisced about his sojourn as a migrant worker in the USA. "What does the English word *stinky* mean?" he suddenly asked me.

"Bad smelling. Why?"

"I was at a party dancing with a gringa. I asked my cousin for some nice flirtatious phrase to say to her. My cousin said, 'Stinky!' I said that to the gringa, and she refused to dance with me anymore."

There was a rustle in the bushes.

A guy got to his feet and drew a pistol. Another guy went to the cab of the pickup, and a third to the cab of the truck. They flicked on the lights to reveal a German shepherd.

BANG! The guy with the pistol fired—up in the air, to scare the dog, which ran away. "It belongs to a rancher near here," he told me.

Twenty minutes later, the bushes rustled again. The guys flicked on the lights of the trucks. It was the fox! He sprang away. The lights went out.

Twenty minutes later, rustle-rustle. On went the lights. The fox again! He sprang away. Lights out.

Twenty minutes later, rustle-rustle. On went the lights. This time, the fox was much closer to us, twenty-five feet away. He was standing with the whole length of his body perpendicular to our line of sight, holding perfectly still, looking over his right shoulder at us, in a pose like that of the Sorcerer at Les Trois Frères.

Every one of us could see the fox. Except the guy with the pistol.

"Shoot him! *Shoot him!*"

"Where is he?"

"Right there!"

"Where?"

"There! Right in front of us! *Shoot him!"*

"I can't see him!"

"He's right there! Look where I'm pointing!"

"I can't see him!"

After half a minute, the fox finally high-tailed it back into the woods. Pistol Guy squeezed off a shot, but, of course, it went wide.

Shaking our heads in disbelief, we sat back down beside the fire. The guy with the pistol talked about how Huichol *brujos*—witches—knew how to transform themselves into foxes. It seemed like an excuse. But the fox had presented himself to us as if he knew he was invisible to the shooter. Being soft-headed myself—or, as I thought of myself, open-minded—I wondered if the fox—which was, in my mind, still, indisputably, a fox—might not also have been a bit of a witch.

As I lay staring up at the bright stars, I recalled the wise, intense expression on the face of the first fox I had known, who now lay in a box on a shelf in a walk-in closet at my dad's condominium. My parents' breakup resulted in the separation of Fox and Bunny, my first two stuffed animals. Fox moved to my dad's place while Bunny came with me to my mom's.

My dad once told me that his own dad never touched him. To make up for that, he touched me too much. The first night I stayed over at his new apartment— I was five—he lay next to me, hand on my shoulder, head against mine, smelling of skin, faint after-shave, and pipe tobacco. He must have been telling himself he was doing this to reassure me. Actually, he was reassuring himself. Or searching for something he'd lost. Maybe some trace of my mom, or of his own childhood. I felt responsible for him. With my mom gone, I was in charge of healing the wounded man. For fear of hurting his feelings, I didn't want to tell him to back off. Fox was between us, crushed under his forearm. "Move over, Dad," I said. "You're smooshing Fox." My dad chuckled and moved over and I slept.

Maybe because I was his only kid, his reminder of the happy married life he could have had if he had paid more attention to his wife, his medicine to heal his relationship with his dad, he idolized me. He kept this up for years, praising everything I did, telling me how special I was, how smart, how handsome, though I told him many times to knock it off. Wishing he were stronger, had more backbone, et cetera, I felt myself growing up weak, infected by his weakness. Sometimes I'd push him off with some variant of "Move over, Dad, you're smooshing Fox," but I always felt responsible for him, too. One day just after my suicidal gesture, I found the strength to ask him to find some strength in himself, and several years after that, he was beginning, hesitantly, to do so. The publication of his art appreciation textbook seemed a step in the right direction. Its modest success in community colleges across America meant that Harcourt Brace Jovanovich was even bringing out a second edition.

Around me, men were snoring or sleeping quietly. The wind whooshed the smell of fresh pine across my face. I wondered where the fox was. I reached up my hand, a dark silhouette, closed the fingers to make a paw, and felt the light of the stars.

***

At dawn, I hiked two and a half hours to San Andrés. When I got there, I scouted around for a place to stay—a hotel or something. All the houses looked the same, adobe brick with zinc rooves. Few people were out on the street. One house had a Fanta sign in front of it. I went in. It was indeed a kind of store, but the dusty display

163

case was empty of all but candy and soft drinks. A Huichol woman sat in the back embroidering a blue and green bird on the breast of a white shirt. "Excuse me, can I buy a Fanta?"

Wordlessly, she stood and got me one and accepted two thousand pesos for the lukewarm drink, then returned to her embroidery. I said, "Ma'am, is there a hotel in town?"

"'Hotel,'" she repeated without looking up. She pulled the thread tight, drove the needle in again, and laughed. "'Hotel!'"

I thanked her and went out. On the street, a big Huichol man was showing a top to a little boy. The guy wrapped the string around the top and whizzed it at the ground. The action made him fart like a thunderclap. While the top spun on the dusty street, the man and the boy laughed. I asked the man if he had any idea where I could stay for a few days. He said his uncle sometimes rented a shed with a mattress to visitors. He shook my hand and introduced himself as Jesús Carillo. He added that he was an artist and asked if I wanted to buy a beaded mask. I didn't. I had run through my traveler's checks and had about a hundred bucks in pesos. He brought me to his uncle's place. I was delighted to sleep on an old piece of foam rubber, much softer than the ground. I stayed three days, tantalized by rumors of a peyote ceremony at a place outside of town called Kukutsú Mepá, Ranch of Dreams. Evidently, though, a tourist wasn't welcome there.

So I hung around the artist's place. I watched him do a yarn painting. To a big square of plywood, he applied a thin layer of beeswax, then made a sketch on it with a nail and filled in the sketch with yarn. It looked quite good. The seventy-dollar beaded mask he wanted to sell me—also made using a layer of beeswax—represented the face of God during the time of creation, he told me, when

164

God had lain under the ground at Wirikuta while all beings were born out of his body. Using hexagonal arrangements of beads, the mask illustrated the emergence from the face of God of green peyote plants, orange lizards, multicolored stars, and a green and white thundercloud. Jesús casually dropped into the conversation a myth of the origin of humans: after being born out of the body of God, a snake split open like a pea pod, and there were people inside.

Jesús lived with his two wives and two mothers-in-law and seven children. No wonder he wanted to make a sale. One night I stayed at his place until late, writing a letter to Lily. When I wanted to return to his uncle's shed, I was menaced on the road by the town's half-wild dogs. Jesús and his family were already asleep in the moonlight. They had decided to sleep outdoors that night, and were lying between blankets in their front yard, all twelve of them. I found a child's sleeping bag draped over a barbed wire fence. It would fit my lower half. There was a small space on a blanket and under another blanket that would fit my upper half: it was right at the end of the row of sleepers, next to the youngest son, who was four. In the morning, when we woke up, he and I had a riotously funny conversation made up entirely of the phrase *¿Cómo estás?*—How are you?—bopped back and forth between us like a balloon that wasn't allowed to touch the ground.

On my last night in town, I fell into the company of five Huichol guys who were on pilgrimage. Drinking tequila with straws out of plastic sandwich bags, we talked for an hour until they heard singing and wanted to see what was up. We went walking and found twenty people singing inside the cinderblock walls of a house whose roof hadn't yet been added. A couple had just married and the ceremony was to bless their home. A fire was dancing in front of a shaman who was sitting on a wooden chair.

165

Everyone else was on blankets on the ground. The shaman was doing call and response singing with the others and shaking three wands tipped with hawk feathers and rattlesnake rattles like the ones the Coras had. All the peyote had already been consumed. The shaman beckoned me over to sit next to him and encouraged me to have a swig of José Cuervo tequila. I did. He said, "Another." I did. Then he started singing again. Every twenty or thirty minutes, he would pause to rest and converse; each time, he would demand that I take two more swigs of the Joe Crow. At one point he leapt to his feet and threw the wands like darts across the room, apparently trying to kill evil spirits. A bit later, he sprang to his feet again and fired a pistol three times in the air. Then everyone went outside to determine which piece of trash on the ground—empty potato chip bag, candy wrapper, cigarette pack—the evil spirit had turned into when it had fallen. I joined in the ultimately inconclusive search. Only when I staggered as I urinated did I realize how wasted I was. At dawn, the shaman asked me to fund a case of beer, which I was happy to do, especially because I inherited a chair from the guy who went to make the purchase. I felt good to have survived the night. The shaman went around sprinkling everyone with water with a calla lily. Jesús showed up and I told him I'd buy his mask. It now seemed more valuable than money. When he returned with it and took the money, he told me another myth: the peyote was the first plant, and from it was born the corn plant, and when that grew up, its ear ripened and opened to reveal the first humans. I thought, "Didn't you tell me humans came out from a snake?" But maybe these were simply visions he had had, images from a personal mythology.

For the next eleven hours I lay in a corn crib by the entrance of the village, sifting through rumors of a pickup truck that might be venturing out. My tequila hangover was stunningly powerful. In my backpack, I had the beaded mask of the face of God wrapped in my cleanest dirty shirt, and in my pocket, twenty-one bucks in cash to make it up to the US border. At sunset, the pickup materialized, its bed laden with a cargo whose nature I never learned. Four of us sat in the front. My knees had to be up near my face because there literally wasn't enough leg room for me to put my feet on the floor. The rocky road did its best to shatter my whole body, starting with my rear end. We rode for five hours in the dark until we came to the home of someone somebody knew. They weren't home. We built a bonfire and crashed out next to it. I woke later because the back of my windbreaker was on fire.

One night led to another. For two nights I rode on freight trains. On the first, I could get into a boxcar; on the second, I couldn't, and slept (surprisingly comfortably) on a metal platform outside as dark Mexico rushed past. The night after that, after hitchhiking all day, I slept in a home in a room with two peyote plants on the windowsill. In the last dream before I wake up, I hear music there. I sit up in bed and see two old Huichol men the size of dolls, dressed in feathered hats and white suits with multicolored embroidery. One is pounding on a little drum, the other sawing on a squeaky violin, both of them singing at the top of their voices. When they see me, they laugh, and whoop, and go *Yip! Yip!*

My dad met me in Texas and introduced me to his publisher friends from Harcourt Brace Jovanovich. How grateful I was when he brought me to an all-you-can-eat buffet at a Chinese restaurant. Sweet and sour chicken had never tasted better. We drove north to Ann Arbor. Along the way, I told him a few things about my trip, but he would tense up when I started to talk about shamanism, so I didn't say much about that. It was safer to agree with his comments about the beauty of the orange evening light on a stand of trees against the blue-gray sky.

My mom welcomed me home, a prodigal son in need of a haircut. I learned I was single: Lily had moved in with a tall, handsome black guy my age. *Mazel tov,* I thought. *It's all good.* We made love one last time to say goodbye. I got a job as a barista at the Café Trieste in the center of town and started to save money to go back to Joaquín's place. It was fun working at the café. I gave away coffee to all my friends, and soon I had a lot of friends. When business was slow, I told them about the monkey-eating Waorani, the opium-growing Coras, the peyote-eating Huichols, and the Secoya wizard with his potion that transformed mild-mannered me into a roaring creature of the forest.